Hinduism

Major World Religions Series

Donald K. Swearer, Editor

Hinduism

BY PAUL YOUNGER and
SUSANNA OOMMEN YOUNGER

Argus Communications
Niles, Illinois 60648

PHOTO CREDITS

John W. Allen/CYR COLOR PHOTO AGENCY   cover: top right
B. Bhansali/SHOSTAL ASSOCIATES   21, 41, 45
D. Forbert/SHOSTAL ASSOCIATES   49
GLOBE PHOTOS   9 (top)
M. P. Kahl/BRUCE COLEMAN INC.   cover: bottom right
B. Kapoor/SHOSTAL ASSOCIATES   53
A. Khan/SHOSTAL ASSOCIATES   16, 17
David M. Knipe   9 (bottom), 28, 57, 73
M. Mattson/SHOSTAL ASSOCIATES   cover: bottom left
V. J. Naidu/GLOBE PHOTOS   13
I. Nalawalla/SHOSTAL ASSOCIATES   cover: top left; 25
Ram Panjabi   69
V. Panjabi/SHOSTAL ASSOCIATES   cover: middle right; 64
ROLOC COLOR SLIDES   32 (top and bottom), 61

MAP AND COVER DESIGN
Gene Tarpey

Printed in the United States of America.

Argus Communications
7440 Natchez Avenue
Niles, Illinois 60648

International Standard Book Number 0-913592-96-X

Library of Congress Number 77-82794
0 9 8 7 6 5 4 3 2 1

Contents

Foreword

"The study of religion is the study of mankind." Religion touches the deepest feelings of the human heart and is part of every human society. In modern times religion has been studied by sociologists and anthropologists as a cultural institution. Psychologists see religion as an expression of an inner human need. Philosophers view it as a system of thought or doctrine. Historians consider religion a part of the intellectual and institutional development of a given era.

What is religion? Modern definitions range from "what man does in his solitude" to "an expression of collective identity," and from "man's experience of awe and fascination before a tremendous mystery" to "projective feelings of dependency." The scope of life that religion is identified with is so vast, and the assumptions about the nature of religion are so varied, that we may readily agree with those who say that the study of religion is the study of mankind.

Religion takes many forms, or perhaps it would be better to say that there are many aspects to religion. They include *belief* (e.g., the belief in a creator God), *ritual action* (e.g., making offerings to that God), *ethical action* (following God's law), the formation of *religious communities,* and the formulation of *creeds and doctrinal systems.*

Joachim Wach, a scholar of religion, has pictured religion in terms of religious experience which expresses itself in thought, action, and fellowship.[1] In this view religion is rooted in religious experience, and all other aspects of religion are expressions of that experience. For example, the Buddha's experience of the highest Truth (in Buddhism called *Nirvana*) led him to teach what he had experienced (known as *dharma*) and resulted in the formation of a monastic community (known as *sangha*).

It must be remembered that religions develop within particular historical and cultural traditions and not in a vacuum. This fact has several profound consequences for the study of religion. In the first place it means that religion can never be completely separated from particular historical and cultural traditions. For example, early Christian thought was deeply influenced by both Semitic and Greek traditions, and such central Christian celebrations as Christmas and Easter owe their form to pre-Christian European traditions.

---

[1]Joachim Wach, *The Comparative Study of Religions* (New York: Columbia University Press, 1958).

Furthermore, since a religion is subject to cultural and historical influences, its traditions are always developing relative to particular times and places. For example, the form of worship used in the Buddhist Churches of America (founded in the late nineteenth century) has as much or more in common with American Protestant worship services than with its traditional Japanese form. A religion, then, as part of a specific historical and cultural stream, changes through time and can be fully understood only in relationship to its historical and cultural forms. By way of generalization we might say that Christianity as a religion is only partially understood in terms of its central beliefs and that a fuller or more complete understanding demands a knowledge of its worldwide history and the influence of its various cultural traditions.

In the second place, since a religion develops within particular historical and cultural settings, it also influences its setting. In other words, there is a give-and-take relationship between a religion and its environment. For example, in traditional societies like medieval Europe, Christianity was the inspiration for much of the art and architecture. The same is true for traditional India, where Buddhism and Hinduism decisively affected artistic forms, or for traditional Persia with Islam. Of course, religion influences its environment in other than merely artistic realms. It has had profound effects on modes of behavior (ethics), conceptions of state (politics), forms of economic endeavor—indeed, on all aspects of life.

As a consequence of the pervasive influence of religion in so many aspects of human endeavor, students of religion and society have observed that in traditional societies religion was never isolated. That is, nothing within the given society was perceived as nonreligious or profane. Every meaningful act was seen as religious or sacred. Professor Robert Bellah of the University of California at Berkeley argues that in the West the split between the sacred and the profane or the differentiation of religion from other aspects of life did not really begin until about the time of the Protestant Reformation. He refers to that period as "early modern." Beginning with the early modern period onward to the present, religion has become more and more differentiated from Western culture. Thus, for example, it is no longer assumed that an American is a Protestant, whereas it is still largely assumed that a Thai is a Buddhist.

The question has been asked, "Can someone understand a religion in which he or she does not believe?" As the previous discussion of the nature of religion indicates, belief in the truth claims of a religious tradition is not a prerequisite for engaging in its study or even for understanding (i.e., making sense of) its beliefs and historical forms. The study of religion, however, does demand empathy and sympathy. To engage in the study of another religion for the purpose of proving that one's own is superior can only result in a distorted understanding of that tradition. Or, for that matter, if one who professes no religious belief approaches the study of religion with an inhibiting skepticism, then the beauty and richness of religion will be lost. For the believer, the study of another religious tradition should enhance his or her own faith-understanding; for the nonbeliever (i.e., agnostic), the study of religion should open up new dimensions of the human spirit.

The objective study of religion should be undertaken because of its inherent significance—because the understanding of cultures and societies, indeed, of humankind, is severely limited when such study is ignored. The study of our own tradition from its own particular creedal or denominational perspective is justifiably a part of our profession of faith. However, such study should not close us off from a sympathetic understanding of other religious traditions. Rather, such inquiry should open us to what we share in common with other religious persons, as well as to what is genuinely unique about our own religious beliefs and traditions.

Is the study of religion relevant today? The authors of this series believe the answer is a resounding "Yes!" The United States—indeed, the world—is in the midst of a profound transition period. The crisis confronting nations today cannot be reduced merely to economic inflation, political instability, and social upheaval. It is also one of values and convictions. The time has passed when we can ignore our crying need to reexamine such basic questions as who we are and where we are going—as individuals, as communities, and as a nation. The interest in Islam on the part of many American blacks, experimentation with various forms of Asian religions by the "Age of Aquarius" generation, and a resurgence of Christian piety on college campuses are particular responses to the crisis of identity through which we are currently passing.

The serious study of religion in the world today is not only legitimate but necessary. Today we need all of the forces we can muster in order to restore a sense of individual worth, moral community, and value direction. The sympathetic study of religion can contribute toward these goals and can be of assistance in helping us to recover an awareness of our common humanity too long overshadowed by our preoccupation with technological and material achievement. As has been popularly said, we have conquered outer space at the expense of inner space.

But why study non-Western religions? The reason is quite simple. We no longer live in relative isolation from the cultures of Asia and Africa. As a consequence the marketplace of ideas, values, and faiths is much broader than it used to be. We are in contact with them through popular books and the news media, but for the most part our acquaintance is superficial at best. Rather than looking at the religions imbedded in these cultures as quaint or bizarre—an unproductive enterprise—we should seek genuine understanding of them in the expectation of broadening, deepening, and hopefully clarifying our own personal identity and direction. The study of religion is, then, a twofold enterprise: engaging the religion(s) as it is, and engaging ourselves in the light of that religion.

The Argus Communications Major World Religions Series attempts to present the religious traditions of Judaism, Christianity, Islam, Hinduism, Buddhism, China, and Africa in their unity and variety. On the one hand, the authors interpret the traditions about which they are writing as a faith or a world view which instills the lives of their adherents with value, meaning, and direction. On the other hand, each volume attempts to analyze a particular religion in terms of its historical and cultural settings. This latter dimension means that the authors are interested in the present form of a religious tradition as well as its past development. How can Christianity or Judaism speak to the problems confronting Americans today? What are some of the new religions of Africa, and are they displacing traditional beliefs and world views? Can Maoism be considered the new religion of China? Is traditional Hinduism able to cope with India's social, economic, and political change? The answers to such questions form a legitimate and important part of the content of the series.

The author of each volume is a serious student and teacher of the tradition about which he or she is writing. Each has spent considerable time in countries where that religious tradition is part of the culture. Furthermore, as individuals, the authors are committed to the positive value the proper study of religion can have for students in these times of rapid social, political, and economic change. We hope that the series succeeds in its attempt to present the world's religions not as something "out there," a curiosity piece of times past, but as a subject of study relevant to the needs of our times.

Introduction

To most North Americans, India seems both strange and fascinating. An Indian in North America is often asked, "How are things in India? Are they getting any better?" "Does the caste system still exist?" "Is it true that people still worship the cow?" "Do you practice yoga?" Although it is true that the cultures of North America and India are very different from one another, the people who live within these cultures are in many ways the same, have many of the same concerns, ask many of the same basic questions.

During the summer of 1974 when we, the authors, were beginning to think about this book, we spent some time at Mahabalipuram, a small town on the southeast coast of India. Walking along the beach in the early morning, we saw three boys hurrying after one another toward the temple in the distance. They were probably in their early teens and were clad only in abbreviated white *dhotis,* or small cloths wrapped about their waists. Each carried a bowl made of a coconut shell suspended from a string. We were curious to know what was in those bowls and so, after some hesitation, we asked one of the boys. Barely stopping, and with only the slightest trace of impatience, he replied that it contained crabs. He picked one up—a small, translucent creature with a string attached. He said that the crabs dig into the sand and catch earthworms which are then used in fishing. Indicating the temple ahead, where we could hear singing, he explained that ordinarily the fishing boats would have gone out by now, but his parents had been to an all-night festival in the temple. Now they and the other fishermen would have to work fast to get the boats out before it became too hot. He said it was his *dharma* (duty)[1] to have the worms ready. We wondered about the boy's schooling, his parents, that temple festival, the livelihood of those fishermen, the organization of life in the cluster of huts that made up the boy's village, and the kind of arrangements that would be made for his marriage. There was no time to ask him about all those things, but we knew a lot about similar boys and could make some reasonable guesses as to what his answers would have been.

That same evening, back in the city of Madras, we went to a restaurant in the busy center of town. The entrance was an outside stairway off which ran a verandah lined with curio shops. In a secluded corner of this verandah sat a woman begging for alms. She was

---

[1]See pages 37–38, where the concept of *dharma* is discussed in detail.

perhaps fifty. Her wavy dark hair, graying at the temples, was tied in a neat bun at the back. Her *sari*—the standard dress of Indian women, made up of six yards of cloth carefully wrapped around the body—was faded but clean. We gave her a bit of money and then, admiring her dignified and peaceful demeanor, asked if she did not have any children who would care for her. She smiled. "I have a son," she said with pride, "but I visit him and his family only on festival days when I can take some presents to the grandchildren. They have often asked me to stay with them. But I don't mind it here. People are kind. They don't drive me out. I have a mat on which I sleep. It is my *karma phalam* (the fruit of my deeds in a previous birth)[2] to be here." And then she concluded, "I enjoy the peace of mind I have, and also my freedom." What an interesting woman! She was a true philosopher. All through dinner the words "fruit of my deeds," "peace of mind," and "freedom" kept ringing in our ears.

These are the people of India. Their teenagers and grandmothers are in some ways like teenagers and grandmothers anywhere. But as they talk about their life, they often say things which seem both fascinating and strange to someone from another culture. This book is an attempt to interpret the religious life of India in such a way that what at first seems fascinating and strange will begin to make sense to the reader.

Interpretation is a job which is more difficult than it appears at first. It requires three interested parties: the speakers, the listeners, and what might be called the "go-betweens."

Through much of their history Indians had little contact with the outside world and never thought of formulating their faith so that others could understand it. They had no concept such as "Hinduism"[3] and no religious authority such as a church or missionary organization which could speak for them. In recent centuries this situation has changed. India now has extensive contact with the outside world and is hesitantly beginning to speak about itself. It still has no one spokesman, however, so it is necessary to listen to many different voices, or speakers, and carefully sort out and piece together their message.

Not very long ago the only questions North Americans asked Indians were those which reflected an unthinking sense of superiority

---

[2]See pages 33–35, where the idea of rebirth is discussed under the heading *"Samsara."*

[3]This term was invented by Western scholars within the past few centuries. The word *Hindu,* like the word *India,* is derived from the name of the Sindhu or Indus River, which is the first major landmark as one approaches the subcontinent from the West. Foreigners designated all the lands beyond the Indus River as *India.* Traditional Indians still refer to their land as *Bharat,* after the name of the first legendary emperor. Most modern Indians now use the terms *India* and *Hinduism.*

and missionary zeal, such as why India has numerous gods and so many "strange" social customs. Then in the sixties came a wave of interest in mysticism and Eastern religions, and Indians were invited to explain their ideas and practices. What came after these two waves seems to be a rather happy mixture of the two. As the questions at the beginning of this Introduction indicate, the listeners now seem both fascinated and skeptical. That is a combination that should make for active and discerning listeners.

The start of a conversation between religious Indian people and North Americans is bound to be a bit awkward. North Americans have certain questions in mind, but Indians want to describe things in their own way. For this reason we, the authors, will act as go-betweens in attempting to present the religious tradition of India as much as possible as an Indian would see it, while at the same time trying to keep in mind the questions which the reader will want answered.

Indians see their religious heritage as having three relatively distinct parts. First, there are the many *traditions* through which individual families and castes [4] in their particular regions of India feel a part of the all-India heritage from the past. Second, there are the *ideas* of great religious teachers which Indians explore in an attempt to find a way to formulate a view of life and to attain salvation. And finally there are the *practices* through which each Indian joins with others in expressing his or her understanding of life. Our study of Hinduism will follow these three perspectives, with Part I on traditions (history), Part II on ideas (philosophy), and Part III on practices (life).

NOTE ON PRONUNCIATION

The Sanskrit words in this book are transliterated in a way which more or less reflects their English pronunciation. In other words, they should be pronounced pretty much as they appear to the reader of English.

To simplify the task of transliteration, we have written two Sanskrit letters as "sh" and two as "ch." In some other books you may find these letters distinguished, so that "Shiva" will appear as "Śiva," "Kshatriya" as "Kṣatriya," "chit" as "cit," and so forth.

The vowel which we have written "ri," as in *Rig Veda*, might be found in other books as "ṛ," or *Ṛg Veda*.

We also have not distinguished between long and short vowels; thus we write *Ramayana*, while in other books you might find *Rāmāyana*.

Paul Younger and Susanna Oommen Younger

---

[4]The concept of caste is discussed more fully on pages 10–12.

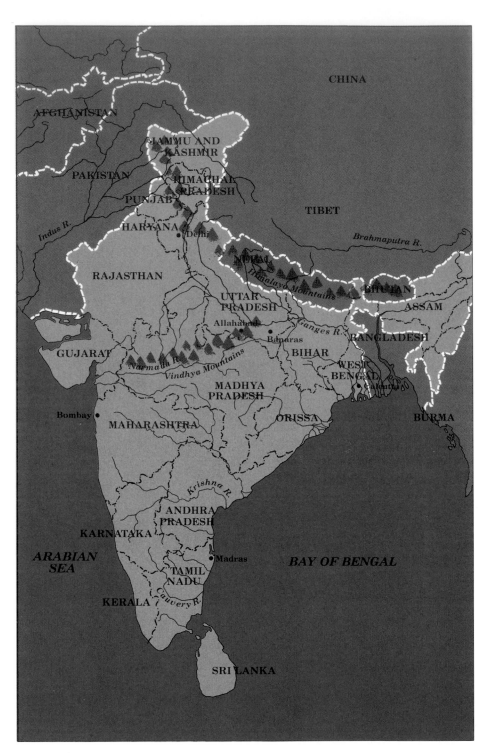

Part I

Traditions

In some religions the primary emphasis is on the set of beliefs which a person or a group holds. In Hinduism, however, the primary emphasis is on the traditions which define the Indian people's way of life. Indian religion is closely associated with traditions about the land, social system, and ancient history of the country.

THE LAND

The Indian subcontinent, of which the modern nation of India forms the major part, is one of the most distinctive major landmasses on earth. It is clearly bounded on all sides, with the Himalaya Mountains in the north and oceans surrounding the other sides. The basically triangular shape of the subcontinent stands out clearly on any map and has led Indians to think of the land itself as a female figure that they refer to as "Mother India." The small countries which surround modern India (Afghanistan, Pakistan, Nepal, Bangladesh, Burma, and Sri Lanka) are all part of the subcontinent; but they were always the

This map of India shows some of the major rivers,
mountain ranges, and cities, as well as the major states.

frontier areas of Indian culture and have each developed religious and political loyalties somewhat different from those of India.

The Indian subcontinent is, for the most part, a richly fertile plain. The southern tip of the triangle is only eight degrees north of the equator, and in many areas the temperature goes up to 120° F (49° C) during certain months, never dropping below freezing except in a few mountainous areas. Because the subcontinent is mostly a uniform plain, the mountains and rivers which mark off that plain are very noticeable. They are considered so important by the Indians that they are almost all designated as being sacred in one way or another.

The most important mountains are the Himalayas (*hima* meaning "snow" and *alaya* "abode"), which mark off the northern boundary of the subcontinent. They are the highest mountains in the world and are the source for the three major river systems of northern India. Draining to the east out of the mountains is the Brahmaputra River, which eventually turns south and empties into the Bay of Bengal. Draining out of the central section, initially toward the west but then southward into the plains and back to the east, is the network of rivers which eventually flow together as the Ganges. In the northwest, five rivers come out of the mountains and cross the northern plain before flowing together to form the Indus. The northwest is where the Himalayas have proved passable and where India has traditionally had contact with other Asian civilizations. While the mountains in the northeastern corner of the subcontinent are not as high as those in the north, they are covered with thick forests due to the heavy rainfall in that area, and they tend to cut Burma off from the rest of the subcontinent.

Elsewhere in the subcontinent, the mountains and rivers have a less dramatic impact on the plain than they do in the north. Dividing the great Ganges plain from the smaller plains farther south are the Vindhya Mountains. These rise to only four thousand feet, but they have been given the legendary role of providing a home for demons and wild creatures, thus serving as a clear psychological boundary between north and south within the subcontinent. Where the Narmada River drains westward into the Arabian Sea and the Krishna, Godavari, and Cauvery rivers eastward into the Bay of Bengal, rich agricultural societies arose. The dry plateau land on the western side of the peninsular part of the triangle and the tropical forests in the mountains on the southwest coast provide for forms of agriculture somewhat different from that in the prevailing plain.

For the most part, the land throughout the subcontinent is fertile and the temperature allows for the growing of crops the year round, provided water is available. Most of the rain is controlled by the monsoon, a periodic wind that sweeps across the land from the Arabian Sea, south and west of the subcontinent. After the hottest summer months (April and May), huge black monsoon clouds move onto the Indian subcontinent, causing heavy rainfall from June through August. (There is a mild version of the monsoon out of the southeast in November and December.) Quite a bit of the early monsoon strikes the mountains of the southwest coast, making it lush and fertile. But much of the rest passes across the western areas of the subcontinent and falls in the northern plain, with the heaviest rain falling in the northeastern corner. Where the monsoon provides over forty inches of rain, one crop can be harvested in September, another in January, and sometimes a third in April.

Indians see deep religious significance in their land. Trees, rocks, and waterfalls are often turned into sacred shrines after people find religious meaning in their presence. Villagers give thanks for the fertility of the soil through rituals and festivals in honor of the goddesses of fertility and prosperity. Mountains and forests provide scenes for the great struggles between divine and demonic forces. People who have developed spiritual power through self-discipline often make pilgrimages to these mystical regions in order to attain greater religious knowledge and spiritual joy.

But for most people, it is primarily the rivers which bring comfort and spiritual life. The holy Ganges, in particular, comes out of the mountains and carries spiritual life as well as life-giving water all across the northern plain of India. Hundreds of thousands of people from all parts of India go to its banks daily to sip its water and cleanse themselves. At the great Kumbha Melas,[1] when the astrological signs are particularly good, millions and millions of people gather to bathe and worship in the largest religious gatherings anywhere in the world. The sacred city of Banaras sits on the banks of the Ganges. It is considered the most auspicious place to die because, after cremation, one's ashes may be floated out on the holy river.

Within the Indian subcontinent are a number of distinct regions, each with its own language and customs and even some of its own religious ideas and practices. Because agricultural people tend to remain on their own land, there has not been much movement of population within India. In spite of a long history as neighbors, the regional subcultures remain surprisingly different from one another even today.

---

[1] Kumbha Melas are special festivals held about every twelve years. These are discussed further on page 65.

The four southern states of Kerala, Tamil Nadu, Karnataka, and Andhra Pradesh probably represent the oldest continuous cultures in the subcontinent. They were far away from the pressures of conquerors and immigrants who usually entered India from the northwest. Their four languages are from what is called the Dravidian family of languages and are rather different from the Indo-European-related languages of the rest of the country. Local kings in the south often invited teacher-priests[2] from the north into their temples and courts. Thus the present cultures of these states are mixtures of older southern traditions and newer traditions borrowed from the north. Christianity came to the coast of Kerala in the early centuries of the Christian Era, and Christians now make up an important segment of the population of that state.

The two western states of Maharashtra and Gujarat are mixtures of conservative agricultural traditions and newer influences due to their proximity to the northwest gateway. In Gujarat the medieval sea trade with Arab peoples gave rise to the most important merchant class of India.

The northwestern states of Himachal Pradesh, Punjab, Haryana, and Rajasthan were traditionally frontier areas where invaders fought and immigrants settled. Punjab is now the home of most of the Sikhs, who practice an independent religion with roots in both Hinduism and Islam.

The large northern states of Uttar Pradesh, Madhya Pradesh, and Bihar comprise the area which is traditionally thought to be the heartland of India. The people of these states all speak Hindi, which has been declared the national language (although there are fifteen "official" languages, with the government in each state using the predominant language of that region).

The eastern states of Orissa, West Bengal, Assam, and some small hill-tribe states were the last area of India to become agricultural. This region has heavy rainfall, numerous streams, and thick jungles on the mountainsides. Some of the early kings of Bengal brought in relatively large numbers of teacher-priests, civil servants, and medical people to teach the local people how to organize an agricultural society. The

---

[2]See discussion of these on page 12.

*India encompasses a diversity of geographic features,
as shown by these two very different scenes.*

result is that the descendants of these groups have become a social and intellectual elite which has played a major role in the modernization of India in recent centuries.

Within these different regions the culture emphasis is often unique to that area. The complex temple ritual of Tamil Nadu, the songs of the saints of Maharashtra, the Sikhism of the Punjab, the northerner's recitation of the epic of Rama, and the Bengali love for the goddess Kali are all unique to their respective areas. But despite the diversity of traditions associated with the different regions, there are many traditions which Indians share in common. It is to these common traditions we now turn.

THE SOCIAL ORDER

The most distinctive feature of Indian culture is the system of social organization known as caste. Although the Indian government has outlawed certain aspects of the caste system, it is still an integral part of Indian society. For this reason, and in order to understand the influence of caste on India's history, it is necessary to learn something about this unique social system. The basic principle of the caste form of social organization is that society is made up of a network of interdependent parts. Each part is like a miniature society with its own occupation, marriage arrangements, and other customs. But all the parts together are arranged in a hierarchical order which, when taken together, constitutes a complete and meaningful social whole.

The basic component of this system is the *jati* (birth group). A *jati* usually consists of about a thousand families which share the same general occupation and customs and arrange all marriages within the group alone. The identity which people share with members of their *jati* has many important religious overtones. The marriage ceremony[3] itself has important religious dimensions. Daily household ceremonies such as the preparation and eating of food, the visits to the prayer room, and the mother's lighting of the evening lamp are carried out according to customs shared in commom by members of the *jati*. Customs associated with particular occupations such as the blessings of a craftsman's tools, the start of plowing, or the opening of a business are all worked out in ways that become traditional in each *jati*. The *jati* is in many ways an extension of the family; it provides the basic religious and social environment in which a child develops.

---

[3]This will be discussed further on pages 70–72.

While to a child the *jati* may at times seem like a world unto itself, its adult members are keenly aware of the *jati*'s interdependence with other *jatis*. The families of a *jati* living in a particular village know that their occupation is only one of the dozen or more which are essential to the well-being of the village. Each of these occupational groups within the village must of necessity have carefully defined relationships with others if all are to function in harmony. In most villages the inter-*jati* relationships are organized around a *jati* of landholders who are accepted as the dominant group in the village. Landholding families have more or less permanent arrangements with families of carpenters, blacksmiths, barbers, washermen, and laborers which bind them to supply things like food and clothing to those families in return for the particular occupational skills which those families offer. The different craft families, in turn, have supplementary arrangements to supply their skills where needed to one another. This network can become very complex in large villages and has a particularly interesting political side to it where a village has two or more landholding *jatis* which over the centuries compete for the dominant position and the loyalty of the service *jatis*. But even where there is competition, the village usually thinks of itself as an economically self-sufficient unit; it is usually united in worshiping the village goddess who brings prosperity and in celebrating the seasonal festivals which mark the agricultural year. In this sense the village is a religious unit for certain purposes, even as the *jati* is for other purposes.

The relationships between any two groups are not, however, confined to their economic interdependence. The final arrangement of groups is hierarchical. Each *jati* thinks of itself as either higher or lower on the social scale than every other *jati*. At the local village level, the hierarchy is expressed by distinguishing between the *jatis* one considers ritually "clean" and with which one could theoretically dine (that is, one considered higher than one's own) and those one considers ritually "unclean," with which one will not eat because they are considered lower. In practice people do eat with those a bit higher or a bit lower than themselves, but certainly not with those who are considered very unclean because their occupation involves the touching of carcasses (leather workers) or dead parts of the body (barbers or washermen).

Outside of the village, where the meeting of "clean" and "unclean" occupational groups is less of an everyday issue, the hierarchy is usually expressed in terms of the general status of a group. For this purpose the thousands of *jatis* are grouped into large occupational classes *(varnas)*, each of which is given a specific place in the hierarchy.

According to Manu,[4] the top three rungs in this hierarchy are special, with the third reserved for merchants (Vaishyas), the second for rulers (Kshatriyas), and the first for teacher-priests (Brahmins). While all other classes can worship and try to improve their fortunes, the chances are that they are too far from the highest form of human existence to achieve salvation in this life. Their hope is that through their worship and good behavior they will be reborn into one of these three classes.

The effect of this hierarchical arrangement of society on the religious hopes of people is that all see themselves as climbing slowly through the hierarchy of being until they finally reach the highest levels of society and an opportunity for salvation. The Brahmins, though often poor, are looked up to and admired not only as those who hold the highest position in society but also as leaders on the path to salvation. The hierarchy of status and respect is based, not on power or wealth, but on a set of ideals which define the stages on the ladder to salvation.

Set outside the social order altogether is a special class of religious wanderers. These people (mostly men, although there are a few women) usually spend most of their time in the forests living off the wild fruit and grains. Occasionally they come to temples and festivals where they receive gifts. People tend to fear them, for they smear their bodies with ash and wear few, if any, clothes. But people also respect them for the great spiritual power they are thought to have stored up. Some of them become religious wanderers as young people and are known as *sadhus,* or people who spend their whole life on religious pilgrimage. Others are retired people who take vows and go on religious pilgrimage or into a full forest existence in their final quest for salvation. They do this because in the lawgiver Manu's view, the life of the higher classes should be divided into four stages: that of the student *(brahmacharin),* the householder *(grihastha),* the forest wanderer *(vanaprastha),* and the saint *(samnyasin).* These religious wanderers, while standing outside the social order, are nevertheless the final confirmation of the hierarchical nature of that order. They are an indication that all people must both respect and seek to emulate the human models that are closest to the state of salvation.

---

[4]In Hindu mythology, Manu was the first man and an important lawgiver.

A Hindu holy man, or sadhu.

While there are many religious rituals which draw the Indian people close to the land, and others which hold them in their social group, most of the myths and rituals of the tradition are directed to the past. The following subsection looks at this sense of past history.

THE HISTORY

Origins

There are two distinct roots which underlie the Indian religious tradition. One is the ancient Indus civilization, discovered by archaeologists within this century and so named because some of the largest cities found so far were along the Indus River. The other is the Rig Vedic civilization of the people who moved into 'India from the northwest sometime about 1500 B.C.

As early as 3000 B.C. the Indus civilization seems to have been highly sophisticated, with elaborate cities supported by a flourishing agricultural economy. The writing on bale-stamping seals which have been uncovered has not yet been deciphered, but from the art found on the seals and elsewhere it is possible to guess something of the religious life of the people. As one might expect in an agricultural society concerned with the fertility of the soil, the most common objects of worship seem to have been the numerous simple clay figurines of fertility goddesses. There are also interesting human and animal figures on the seals, a few beautifully carved dancing figures, and an impressive-looking bearded man who may have been a king or an ascetic or both. Differing interpretations have been made of these figures, but the only things we can be certain of are that the people worshiped fertility goddesses and were part of an authoritarian society which, among other things, insisted on carefully designed streets and drains.

The Rig Vedic civilization did not leave any archaeological remains that have been discovered; but it did leave a magnificent hymn book called the *Rig Veda,* which was composed in an early form of the Sanskrit language. The hymns reflect a vigorous and even boisterous nomadic society in which people cried out to their favorite god as they headed into battle, rejoiced at the rising of the sun, joined together in assembly, and felt lonely on a quiet evening. Some of the hymns may have been composed when the Vedic people were still nomads in Central Asia, but most were probably composed after they began to settle down on the Indian plain.

The hymns are usually addressed to a single deity, but there are several dozen different deities addressed in the collection as a whole. The most popular of the deities is Indra, a hot-tempered warrior who defeats the enemy Vritra and who also established the world. He is the subject of the following hymn.

Who, the new born, the foremost, the one of spirit, the god
　　Who surpassed the rest of the gods with his might;
From the puffing of whom by the greatness of his manliness
　　The Heaven and Earth trembled,
He, O men, is Indra.

Who fastened the quivering earth,
　　Who set at rest the moving mountains,
Who stretches out wide the atmosphere,
　　Who propped up the heaven,
He, O men, is Indra.

Who by slaying the dragon set free the seven rivers,
　　Who drove out the cows in the cave of Vala,
Who begot the fire between the clouds,
　　The victor in battles,
He, O men, is Indra.

Some of the hymns are less boisterous than those addressed to Indra and seem to have been written in the context of an elaborate sacrificial fire ritual. Many of these hymns are addressed to fire (Agni) itself.

I call upon Agni, the official priest of the sacrifice,
The god who is the ministering priest and singing priest as well,
The one who lavishly bestows wealth.

Agni is to be praised by heroes of old,
And also of those today,
May he conduct the gods here.

Both the Indus and the Rig Vedic civilizations were destined to make major contributions to the Indian culture that later developed. The general framework of the Indus civilization as an agricultural society which put great stress on order and the worship of fertility goddesses has certainly continued in India to this day. Scholars are not agreed on whether more specific symbols on the bale-stamping seals preview the religious meaning later associated with the bull or the god Shiva. But that, too, is quite possible. The language of the *Rig Veda* eventually became the language of scholars and priests throughout India, and in this sense its conceptions about the gods and the order of the cosmos had a strong influence on all later Indian thought. Gods such as Indra

The pottery shown above and the clay toys on the right are excavated remains of the Indus civilization.

and Agni are not the major deities of later Hinduism, nor is fire sacrifice the central ritual, but all are recognized and play an important part in the tradition as a whole.

The Indian tradition looks on the period of its origins with awe. Although it is a period about which little is known, it is reverenced as a foundation of truth. "The Veda" is accepted by the later traditions as *shruti* (that which is heard) and is given a special place of sacredness exceeding the respect accorded the later tradition, which is known by the lesser title of *smriti* (that which is remembered). While only a few Indians today can understand the language of the hymns of the *Rig Veda,* they are still recited in rituals to serve as a reminder of the sacred source from which all the truth of the tradition is derived.

The Period of Creative Formulation

Sometime about the sixth century B.C., serious philosophical ferment stirred India and resulted in the clear formulation of the major ideas of the Indian tradition. This formulation took place in two different settings. The teachings of the Buddha and the Mahavira were preserved and promulgated by the monastic orders known as Buddhism and Jainism respectively. The semi-secret teachings which came to be known as the *Upanishads* were circulated by Upanishadic teachers of the Vedic heritage.

The life story of the Buddha was from early times a popular favorite. Raised as a prince, he was pampered by the court and married a beautiful maiden. Soon after the birth of his son he began to venture out into the world where he saw sickness, old age, and death in ways he had never seen them before. After meeting an ascetic, the Buddha vowed that he too would renounce the world of luxury and he left his palace to begin reflecting on the nature of suffering. After seeking the advice of other teachers, he eventually went to sit under a bodhi tree where he received *buddhi* (enlightenment). He then began to teach his Four Noble Truths: (1) All of life is *duhkha,* or painfulness; (2) it is painful because it is transient; (3) there is another kind of reality called Nirvana; and (4) the path of Nirvana has eight steps: right understanding, right intention, right speech, right action, right livelihood, right effort, right mindfulness, and right concentration.

Mahavira's teachings were somewhat similar but more austere. For Mahavira the path to the end of pain involved a severe discipline which first put a stop to all action that produced pain and then sought to rid the individual of the accumulated polluting effect of previous actions. The final result of this path was for the body to be totally purified and freed of the weight of evil—to rise from the world to a permanent state of pure existence.

Both Buddhism and Jainism were eventually declared to be unorthodox by the later Hindu teachers, but these teachings had a major impact on Indian thought and continue to flourish as religious traditions distinct from Hinduism. Buddhism was adopted by the emperor Ashoka of the great Mauryan dynasty which united most of India for the first time in the third century B.C. Missionaries sent out by Ashoka and by later emperors such as Kanishka of the Kushana dynasty took Buddhism to Sri Lanka and to China, from where it continued to spread into Southeast Asia and East Asia. But it eventually lost its foothold at home and almost disappeared from India. Jainism, on the other hand, is an important influence in western India to this day.

In contrast to the dramatic beginnings of the Buddhist and Jain monastic orders, the Upanishadic teachers sought to relate their teachings to the Vedic heritage that had come down from the hymns of the *Rig Veda*. The actual teachings of the *Upanishads* were rather different from those that were implicit in the earlier hymn books. The Upanishadic teachers did not believe either in crying out to the gods or in the ritual of sacrifice. What they sought to do was find the Reality *(Brahman)* that lay behind the order of the cosmos and the activity of the gods. They sought in particular to examine the nature of human consciousness, for they thought that the essence *(atman)* underlying individual consciousness must be the same as the Reality underlying the cosmos.

The Upanishadic teachers shared with the Buddhists and Jains the sense that life must be a quest for a way to overcome the *duhkha,* or pain, which one feels at the transience of life. While the Buddhists and Jains pursued this quest by forming monastic orders which set aside the many local rituals and called for all to follow a single path, the Upanishadic teachers looked on the quest as a form of reflection that was to be carried out within the traditional ritual structure. Even though Buddhism and Jainism proved very popular for some centuries, and even won some measure of royal support, it was the more traditional path of the *Upanishads* which was eventually to prove the central path of Hinduism.

The Age of Consolidation

The centuries following the emergence of the Buddhist and Jain monastic orders in the sixth century B.C. were exciting ones for India. Political fluctuations occurred as the Mauryan dynasty (322–185 B.C.)

brought unity to India and a great Buddhist emperor in Ashoka, followed by a somewhat weaker Hindu dynasty called the Shungas (185–72 B.C.). The Kushanas (A.D. 78–250), who were Buddhists, ruled in the northwest until the Hindu Guptas (A.D. 320–540) put together a stable empire which covered most of North India. Intellectually, too, things were in a flux. Although the Buddhists and Jain orders were very popular and the Upanishadic teachers were respected, many local traditions flourished as well. Sometime during the period, two epics which had probably been circulating as local legends began to be accepted as the best overall statement of the Indian view of the world.

In their present form, these two epics are collections of stories—the *Ramayana* making up about five normal-sized volumes and the *Mahabharata* probably fifteen or twenty. But in their original forms they were not so much collections of stories as thoughtful attempts to come to grips with the problems of chaos and disorder in human life and to set forth how it was that order and purpose would eventually prevail. The basic thesis of the epics is that history is divided into cycles, in which the world starts in pure righteousness or order *(dharma)* and then goes through four ages *(yugas)* in which righteousness gets weaker and weaker until it becomes necessary for the gods to destroy the world and start again. Thus it may be painful for a king to see righteousness being destroyed; but his ability to find meaning and purpose through that disorder constitutes his greatness.

The *Ramayana* is said to have taken place at the end of the second *yuga,* an age when righteousness was basically intact even though seriously threatened. Rama, the prince and heir apparent of Ayodhya, is sent into exile in the forest for fourteen years because his father's second wife wants *her* son rather than Rama to be put on the throne. She had tricked Rama's father into promising her a favor, which she claimed by making Rama an exile. Rama goes into the forest, considered the domain of evil powers called *rakshasas* (demons), along with his lovely wife Sita and his faithful brother Lakshmana. Eventually Sita is abducted by the *rakshasa* king Ravana,[5] and a war ensues in an attempt to rescue her. In this war a friendly society of monkeys is the crucial factor in Rama's success, and the monkey Hanuman emerges as the highest embodiment of devoted and loyal service. Rama, while the personification of righteousness throughout, is sorely tested by the

---

[5]"The Abduction of Sita" is recounted on pages 59–62.

Lord Krishna is being honored at this celebration of his birthday in Bombay.

resourceful and well-equipped *rakshasa* forces. He prevails by a combination of his own faithfulness, his brother's loyalty, and the unexpected help of the monkeys.

The *Mahabharata* story is set at the end of the third *yuga*, and the tragic war it records ushers in the Kali *yuga*, or the final age of disorder and unrighteousness in which we now live. The problem in this case is that two sets of cousins each claim to be the rightful heirs to the throne. In the struggle which ensues the five Pandava brothers eventually prevail, but only after a most tragic and drawn-out war. The drama of the story centers around the different ways in which the five brothers respond to the tragic crisis in which they are involved. The oldest brother, Yudhishthira, hates war and wants to retreat from the world in the manner of the Buddhists and Jains. The second brother, Bhima, is a belligerent fellow who thinks about little except getting on with the battle. The fourth and fifth brothers are twins and somewhat young and naive. The story concentrates on the third brother, Arjuna, who combines the ascetic distaste for war with outstanding skill as a warrior. The high point of the epic is a section called the *Bhagavad Gita* (Song of the Lord) in which Arjuna hesitates before the battle and discusses his doubts with Krishna, who in this context is serving as his friend and charioteer.

After Arjuna expresses his distaste for going into battle against his cousins, Krishna argues that it is precisely because the world is threatened by chaos and disorder that Arjuna must act. Krishna goes on to convince Arjuna that his action need not be that of a passion-filled warrior who would just be creating more chaos. He shows Arjuna that, while disguised as a friend and charioteer, he is really the Lord of the Universe and through him Arjuna can know the order, or *dharma,* of the whole world. In the performance of his own duty *(sva dharma)* as a warrior, Arjuna acts with detachment. For through devotion to Krishna his action has been absorbed into the full *dharma* of the universe. At the end of the discussion, Arjuna is no longer enticed by the option of ascetic withdrawal, and he goes on into the battle; but his inner self has been awakened and his action in the world is now a working out of the realization of his true self. The *Bhagavad Gita,* while just a small chapter in the larger epic, has gradually become the most revered writing in the Indian tradition.

The basic stories of the *Ramayana* and *Mahabharata* were probably current in courtly circles even before the time of the Buddha, but they were rewritten and given new prominence sometime about the beginning of the Christian Era. The philosophy involved seems to have been popular particularly among kings who believed in making sense of life in the world in spite of its difficulties. By the fourth century A.D., the kings of the Gupta dynasty were trying to work out this vision of righteousness, or *dharma,* in all its fullness. Samudra Gupta, the greatest ruler of this dynasty, pictured himself as a *chakra-vartin* (literally, "one who turns the cosmic wheel of dominion") who was destined to bring order to the whole world. His coins picture him as both the military hero riding a horse in triumph and the cultured gentleman playing a musical instrument. He began the building of temples in different parts of his empire and had images of Hindu deities on the reverse of his coins. The Gupta age was later known as the Golden Age of the Hindu tradition, for it was seen to represent the proper balance of religion, culture, and political authority.

The Development of Sectarian Hinduism

With the decline of the Gupta Empire in the fifth and sixth centuries A.D., India became politically decentralized. Strong regional dynasties arose in some areas (Pallavas, Cholas, and Pandyas in the south; Rashtrakutas and Chaulukyas in the center; and Palas and Senas in the east). Local traditions also began to regain prominence. The sectarian religious practices which emerged were an interesting mixture of local myths and rituals, traditions introduced by Brahmin priests, and ceremonies of special interest to the kings (who generally built the temples and sponsored the priests). The texts known as the *Puranas* are the beautiful and yet often chaotic record of this synthetic blending of traditions which took place in the development of sectarian Hinduism. In an attempt to simplify the story of this ever-changing mythological heritage, scholars usually speak of three movements within sectarian Hinduism: that associated with the god Vishnu, that associated with the god Shiva, and that associated with the *shaktis,* or goddesses.

VISHNU

There are old myths about Vishnu, some of which go all the way back to Rig Vedic hymns. In one of these hymns Vishnu, in a dwarf manifestation, covers the earth in two strides and is made Lord of the Universe.[6] Another favorite tells of Vishnu reclining on the coils of the snake, the symbol of chaos, while out of his navel grows a lotus on which sits the god Brahma[7] and others who go about creating the world while Vishnu holds off chaos.

---

[6]See pages 66–67 for an expansion of this story.

[7]The name Brahma is not to be confused with *Brahman* the Absolute or with Brahmins, members of the teacher-priest class.

After temples to Vishnu were built, the myths associated with him began to multiply. One of the ways of incorporating a diversity of myths within one system was the concept of the *avatara,* by which Vishnu was thought to "descend" to earth in times of crisis in whatever form was appropriate to that particular crisis. In this way, for instance, Vishnu took on the popular form of a boar called Varaha in order to dive deep into the primeval mud and rescue Mother Earth (Prithivi) when she was sinking. Using the *avatara* idea the heroes of the two epics, Rama and Krishna, could be seen as forms of Vishnu descended to earth in times of crisis. The Krishna story especially was extended beyond the *Mahabharata* account, with the *Bhagavata Purana* recounting in detail the touching stories of Krishna the mischievous child and Krishna the romantic youth among the cowherd girls.

SHIVA

The Shiva myths may be even older than those of Vishnu, but there seems to have been some hesitancy on the part of the Brahmins about including them all in the tradition. Most of the myths about Shiva picture him as a wild ascetic in the mountains who possesses the power to create but is a bit awesome and hard to approach. One form of his creative power is his dance, which image makers have carefully formulated by placing the drum of creation and the fire of destruction in two of his hands, while another hand indicates the peace which follows creation, and still another points to the gracious kick of the leg which calls for a re-creation of the world once it has been destroyed. The most common representation of Shiva is not in a human form at all; it is as a *linga,* or phallus, which is the symbol of reserved potency or power to create. The stories associated with this symbol usually involve some demonic forces working in the world while Shiva in his mountain retreats stores up his power. In order to make this power effective, his consort Parvati (whose name means "daughter of the mountain") usually has to approach him through some ascetic form of her own, thus giving birth to sons who save the world. Shiva does not, as such, take on different forms as does Vishnu; but through his own mysterious actions and through his consort Parvati and his sons (Skanda the warrior and Ganesha the fat, elephant-headed god of good

Images of Ganesha are often found in Hindu temples and homes. Many Hindus pray to him for success in travel, education, and business.

fortune), he can be either an awesome or a tender presence in a devotee's life.

SHAKTIS

The *shakti,* or goddess, myths were an awkward problem for the Brahmins. Most villages, even today, worship a goddess of fertility, and stories about goddesses are particularly popular among the lower classes in India. The Brahmins were not too keen about circulating myths popular primarily among the lower classes; so the *Puranas* ignored many of these stories and included others by making them stories about consorts of Vishnu and Shiva. But the goddesses never lost their popular role. In Bengal, for instance, stories about the motherly Durga and the fierce Kali were among the most popular.

The emergence of sectarian Hinduism brought new vitality to the links between the local traditions and the tradition of the literate elite. Local deities could now be seen as forms *(avataras)* of Vishnu or consorts or sons of Shiva; and a person could combine a warm devotional *(bhakti)* relationship to a local deity with a profound understanding of the Upanishadic idea of *Brahman,* or Reality. Two of the greatest philosophers of India who emerged late in this period combined devotion with philosophy in just that way. Shankara, who was born in the eighth century, was a devout worshiper of Shiva; but he also set forth a brilliant and complex interpretation of Upanishadic thought called *a-dvaita* (nonduality), in which he argued that *Brahman* alone was real and all else was illusion. Ramanuja, who lived in the twelfth century, was a devout worshiper of Vishnu. He disagreed somewhat with Shankara by arguing that while *Brahman* alone is ultimately real, both the world and the worshiper have some reality at the time of devotion and prior to final liberation.

The decentralization of Indian culture which took place with the development of regional empires and the emergence of a variety of religious sects made India vulnerable to outside pressures. When these pressures took the form of Muslim invaders in the tenth century, Hinduism continued with vitality at the local level but suffered setbacks within the culture as a whole. The following subsection tells the story of the survival of Hinduism during that period.

The Period of Survival: Muslim and British Rule

After two centuries of raids, India in the twelfth century A.D. came under foreign rulers who dominated the country until 1947. The first wave of foreign rule was particularly painful. The Turkish Muslims, who set up the Delhi Sultanate in 1192, were barbarous nomadic tribesmen who tore down temples, burned libraries, and plundered across all northern India. By the time a different Muslim dynasty, the Moguls, took over in the sixteenth century, things had settled down. The great Mogul ruler Akbar attempted to bring about a synthesis of Hindu and Muslim culture which resulted in such glorious monuments as Shah Jahan's Taj Mahal, built in the seventeenth century. But the last of the Moguls, Aurangzeb, was a rigid Muslim. And by the time the British took over in the eighteenth century, many Hindus were fiercely anti-Muslim and the country was in political disarray.

During the long centuries of Muslim rule, Hinduism became a somewhat secretive religion held together primarily by Brahmins who lived in relative poverty and quietly wrote commentaries on the great literary heritage which had developed. From time to time the people were inspired by a popular saint who would, through his unusual life or beautiful songs, bring about a new wave of devotion. Kabir, for example, was a saint who tried to combine Muslim and Hindu ideas; Tulsi Das, a more orthodox Hindu, wrote a popular new version of the *Ramayana* story; and Chaitanya was a saint in Bengal who went into ecstasy singing love songs to Krishna.

Most of the saints were careful to stay away from political involvement. But in Maharashtra, on the west coast, some of the saints were openly critical of the Mogul rulers and they inspired one of the Hindu heroes of the Muslim period. Shivaji was born in the seventeenth century, the son of a Hindu who worked for one of the Muslim provincial rulers. Distressed by the powerless position of his people, Shivaji organized a raiding party which conquered Muslim forts and generally harrassed the Muslim rulers. Although he never reconquered his country, Shivaji's cry for Hindu political power continued to inspire the people of Maharashtra, and his example prompted political leaders in the twentieth century to help awaken India to fight for independence.

The British challenge to Hinduism was more subtle than that of the Muslims. At first the British concentrated on trade; but when the opportunity for political control came their way with the collapse of Mogul power near the end of the eighteenth century, they began to take a hand in Indian affairs. By the beginning of the nineteenth century they had decided that Indian culture was morally inferior and that legislation and English education must be employed in an effort to change the basic ideas and practices of India. At first the Hindu leaders were uncertain how to respond. But they soon entered into the debate and challenged the British arguments directly.

One result of this debate was the emergence of a new kind of public presentation of Hinduism. Early in the nineteenth century Ram Mohun Roy argued that while reforms were needed, they could be made on the basis of Hindu scriptures themselves. By the turn of the century, Vivekananda had carried the debate to the West by attending the World Parliament of Religions in Chicago. There he argued that the philosophy of Vedanta, which was the ancient philosophy of the Upanishads as interpreted by Shankara, could provide the only proper basis for the unity of humanity. While at home in independent India sectarian Hinduism has returned to the older forms of temple ritual, other Hindu teachers have followed Vivekananda's example and have brought special versions of Hinduism to the rest of the world in the form of Transcendental Meditation, the Hare Krishna movement, Divine Light, and so forth.

While Vivekananda and others were challenging the British critique of Indian thought, leaders such as B. G. Tilak and Mohandas K. (Mahatma) Gandhi were arguing that the traditional Hindu bases for social and political action were also sound. Tilak, as a Maharashtrian and a great admirer of Shivaji, argued vehemently at the turn of the century that British legislation on things like marriage regulations showed a total misunderstanding of the Indian social system. He insisted that the British were unfit to rule India and should leave. Mahatma Gandhi tried a subtler technique; he thought that after many centuries of foreign rule it would take Hinduism some time to find a new political form, and he believed that British self-righteousness could be used to India's advantage. By declaring that India would win its freedom by passive resistance alone, he awakened an old Hindu confidence that order, or *dharma,* would prevail. He also forced the British to acknowledge and respect political leadership which, even by their own Christian standards, was exemplary. The result was not only political independence but a reexamined and revitalized religious life which was prepared to tackle the questions of social and political adjustment in a new order.

To the Indian, Hinduism is not just a body of doctrine; it is a total way of life. The word *tradition* calls up associations with a particular

A Hindu temple in Nasik in the western state of Maharashtra. Although some Hindus worship daily in temples, most go only on special occasions and during festival celebrations.

land and a particular society as much as it does with a particular historical heritage. Recent attempts to translate Hinduism into a body of doctrine that can be exported are a radical departure from this traditional pattern and have been only partly successful. Even within its own environment, Hinduism as a total way of life now faces new challenges as cities are built and technology plays a greater and greater role in life. But the Hindu tradition in India has faced serious challenges before and has adjusted to them without losing its basic identity. Its present vitality would seem to indicate that its response to the challenge of technology will be equally successful.

Part II

Ideas

The basic ideas of Hinduism can be seen as answers to three questions: (1) What is the nature of human experience? (2) What is the nature of Ultimate Reality? (3) What is the way to achieve salvation? The Hindu's answer to each of these questions comes in two parts, the first being a general answer and the second a more specific one. The general answer to the question about the nature of human experience is found in the idea of *samsara*,[1] which describes the interrelatedness of all forms of reality through space and time. The more specific answer is found in the idea of *duhkha*, which describes the pain that human consciousness feels when it becomes aware of the transience of everything in life. The general answer to the second question about the nature of Ultimate Reality lies in the concept of *dharma*, which points to the order and structure of the cosmos and the moral life of humanity. The more specific answer comes from the concept of *Brahman* the Absolute unknowable Reality which manifests itself in the gods of human experience. The general answer to the question about how to achieve salvation involves the idea of *yoga*, or the paths by which one seeks salvation. The specific answer lies in the idea of *moksha*, or the final state of liberation itself.

---

[1]It is not possible to provide simple English equivalents for the six words that are italicized in this paragraph, because there are no exact equivalents in Western thought for the ideas they refer to. The six concepts will be discussed in further detail in this section.

31

WHAT IS THE NATURE OF HUMAN EXPERIENCE?

Samsara

The word *samsara* roughly means "that which flows together." It refers to what the Indians consider the wonderful mixture of living and nonliving forms which make up the world around them. Hidden in this concept are three assumptions about life which are unfamiliar to most North Americans.

The first assumption implicit in the concept of *samsara* is that the world has a mysterious "sealike" base which makes the interrelations between various forms of reality (plants and animals, earth and sky, gods and humans) very flexible. While in ancient Hebrew thought there was also an idea of a basic watery chaos, the Creation stories recorded in the first few chapters of Genesis state that this chaos was overcome as God gave everything a more or less fixed place. In India, too, there are many "creation" stories in a sense, but they are actually only stories about the *temporary* reordering or "re-creation" of things within the more basic realm of *samsara*. Life is not defined in terms of a fixed order of relationships between humanity and nature or humanity and God, nor is it defined in terms of a fixed time span beginning with Creation and proceeding to an end. For the Hindu, the world is like a mysterious sea which in itself has no beginning and end and no fixed order.

The second assumption implicit in *samsara* is that many forms of reality "flow together," or influence one another, in the process of constituting the world. The space in which life is lived is shared by animals and plants, fire and water, earth and sky, humans and gods. Transformations from one form to another (for example, "animals" eat "plants" but then die and return to the "earth") continually occur, but all share the same basic environment. The universe is, as it were, closed (like an egg) in that all matter and energy are conserved even though they are continually being transformed into new forms. Human beings cannot indefinitely conquer nature, for everything is cyclical. Excessive activity of one form of life will bring countervailing forces which will restore the overall balance. In the Hindus' favorite image for stories or for paintings, life is like a closed garden in which

Shown here are two typical scenes of life in India—villagers going for water (top) and riding on a bullock cart (bottom).

plants and animals, gods and humans, all romp and play as they share the joys and sorrows of life together. This round of activity is called *lila.*

The third assumption implicit in the concept of *samsara* is that the complex interrelatedness of life not only occurs in space to include different forms of reality but also occurs in time to include a whole series of lives which we as living beings pass through. In other words, the Hindus assume that all living beings are continually reborn in new forms and that the creatures we are at a particular time are in a complex way interrelated with forms which we possessed in the past and will possess in the future.[2] The principle by which one life is related to the next is known as the law of *karma,* which asserts that every action produces its necessary consequences even if the consequences are only realized in subsequent lives. In this sense people are not born with a clean slate upon which personalities are stamped by early sensory experiences; nor are they born with the curse of sin and guilt. All are born with a heritage which is their own from previous lives, and their interrelatedness with that heritage, as well as with the complex forms of reality which surround them, give them the environment in which they work out their lives.

There are three basic attitudes toward life which the Indian derives from the assumptions implicit in the concept of *samsara.* The first is that life is complex and mysterious. The second is that life is warm and reassuring. And the third is that life is transient and therefore frustrating and painful to the self, which looks for meaning within it. This final attitude will lead into the second idea, that of *duhkha.* But prior to that we must consider the mysterious and reassuring aspects of life.

Children born into a world defined as *samsara* are soon mystified. They are taught about all sorts of plants, animals, grandparents and relatives, gods and demons, and lives which they lived before. Because children cannot fully comprehend these teachings, they learn to accept the sense of mystery and to recognize that there is much in the world that they do not control or even fully understand.

While children born into a world defined as *samsara* are mystified, they are also provided with an abundant sense of warmth and reassurance. The plants and animals, grandparents and gods to whom they are introduced are all presented to them as friends in a closed world of joy and fertility. The sense of the world that is learned at a mother's breast is extended to its furthest limit. As mentioned earlier, the land of India is seen as a mother; the rivers are thought of as female and breastlike as

<hr />

[2]Many Westerners use the word *reincarnation* to describe this concept. It is not quite accurate, as it appears to express a doctrine implying a complicated afterlife. Hindus never discuss this idea as a doctrine; they just assume that humans share in the dying and rebirth cycles of nature.

they provide the nourishment for the earth; and Shri, the goddess of the home and prosperity, is distinctively characterized by her full, swelling breasts.

While the mystery and complexity of *samsara* might tend to be overwhelming, the immediate experience of *samsara* is warm, reassuring, and pleasant. The sense of responsibility which is related to the option to obey or disobey God or to the injunction "to go out into the world" and make one's way is not a part of the Hindu experience of the world. They do not think of themselves initially as creatures laden with responsibility, but as forms of life free to revel in the other forms of life around them. To some the warmth eventually proves oppressive, while to others it is a source of vitality and strength. But for all it provides a security and an identity out of which the further dimensions of life can develop.

One of the further dimensions of life among humans is the awareness of selfhood, or consciousness. As the Hindus see it, humans are born within the complex interrelatedness of life known as *samsara,* but they are also born as conscious beings possessing a consciousness which reaches beyond this life. People born as conscious beings not only accept the mystery and warmth of *samsara* but also ask questions about this whole world of experience. In the light of these questions, the experience of being human takes on a second dimension.

Duhkha

The word *duhkha* means "bad experience." It is contrasted with *sukha,* or good experience. For some forms of life, experience is mysterious and reassuring but is not necessarily either good or bad, pleasurable or painful. But for humans, as conscious beings, simple existence is not possible. As conscious beings, humans are required to undergo experiences which are pleasurable as well as those which are painful.

The great contribution of the Buddha to Hindu thought was his analysis of the consciousness of pleasure and pain and his idea that the transience of experience eventually turns all pleasure into pain.

> All is *duhkha*. Sickness is *duhkha*. Old age is *duhkha*. Death is *duhkha*. Having experience which we cherish pass away is *duhkha*. Having experience which we do not cherish is *duhkha*.

To most North Americans, painfulness of experience means the suffering some human beings undergo. But that is a very different concept from *duhkha*. What the Buddha meant by *duhkha* was the universal problem of being conscious of experience. If one thinks of consciousness as something relatively permanent which can be distinguished from the passing scene of experience around it, then it is natural that consciousness should find itself clinging to transient experiences of pleasure only to find them disappearing from its grasp. To consciousness, the experience of transience is necessarily an experience of painfulness.

Duhkha, or the painfulness of life, is only real when viewed from the perspective of consciousness. Life is not ordinarily or directly experienced as painful; but when consciousness becomes aware of itself, it throws the transient experience of the world into a new light. In this sense the concept of *duhkha* is a religious concept which is the first stage in the new awareness of an awakened soul. From the perspective of the road to salvation, human beings see the whole world of *samsara* as an experience of *duhkha,* or pain, from which they must somehow gain release.

Because that from which men seek release is *samsara* itself, Hindu thought does not really have a doctrine of sin or evil as such. There are, of course, numerous demons or evil powers in Indian mythology; and there are examples of people who in their devotion to Shiva or one of the other gods say that they have sinned. But the demons do not represent radical evil in the sense of a power set up in opposition to the highest Reality, nor does the devotee's prayer mean that he or she feels deeply that there is a radical rebellion against God. What spurs people on to seek salvation is not a sense of sin and guilt—a particular aspect of life which needs correction—but the awareness of *duhkha,* or of the inevitable painfulness of all experience when seen from the vantage point of consciousness. Life is painful because consciousness has gotten itself entangled in transience, and it is to the disentangling of those two unsuitable partners that the search for ultimate Reality and the paths of salvation address themselves.

The two Indian answers to the question about the nature of human experience take two very different directions which may on first glance even seem to be contradictory. On the one hand *samsara* or the general scene in which life flows together emphasizes the interrelatedness through space and time of many forms of life and leaves one with an environment which is fascinating and warm. On the other hand the consciousness which becomes aware of that changing scene experiences it as *duhkha* or painfulness and thus sets up the need to seek out and define something else which is Ultimate and Real. Thus we are led to our second question:

WHAT IS THE NATURE OF ULTIMATE REALITY?

Dharma

The word *dharma* comes from the root meaning "to support" or "to connect." *Dharma*, then, is the order which gives structure and purpose to the universe. An individual's relationship to this order is understood as his or her *dharma*, or duty. The cosmos, society, and the individual are all guided by the principle of *dharma*.

The cyclical and unstable domain of *samsara* is not really a cosmos. Within *samsara* the earth is constantly in danger of sinking into the mud of chaos, and various demonic forces are seen as having the power to "swallow" the moon or disrupt the sun from its course. What keeps everything in its place and harmonizes and balances the many forces which make up the cosmos is the order called *dharma*.

The gods, as aspects of the cosmos, are also under the rule of *dharma*. Uncontrolled, the gods might tend to disrupt the harmony of the universe, for in their zeal to combat a particular enemy they are often intemperate. In the Vedic hymns Indra, for example, became vehement and uncontrollable when battling his enemy Vritra. In later mythology Shiva lets the demons run wild as he withdraws into his ascetic concentration and fails to make his consort, Parvati, conceive the son who was expected to control the demons. When Parvati finally awakens him from his trance, he goes to the opposite extreme and is said to have entered into an erotic embrace which lasted "thousands of years." Krishna as a boy teased his mother by snatching the curds or yogurt she was making, and later as a youth he enticed the wives of the cowherds away from their families with his magic flute playing. Hence, the gods in Hinduism are not creators and lawgivers who remain in a supervisory role on the outside of life, as does the Judeo-Christian God. They are passionate participants in life, as were the ancient Greek and Roman gods. And it is only because of the order of *dharma* that their actions can be seen as having an overall meaning and purpose.

Like the cosmos, society too must be ordered by *dharma*. Indian society is not seen as an expression of group power, as are societies in other cultures. The power of various groups is recognized as a factor in social change, but it is thought that the unguided competition of social groups would create even greater chaos than the unguided behavior of heavenly bodies or gods. Society must be guided by the principles of order, or *dharma*, which provide each group with a particular function and a particular set of rituals and behavior patterns appropriate to that function. Thus society is seen as a structured whole which not only operates in peace and harmony but also enables the individual to become aware of the hierarchical order of Reality.

The individual as a member of a family, a *jati* (birth group), a *varna* (occupational class), and a nation learns of rituals, duties, and regulations which are appropriate to him or her as a member of each of these groups. Through these directives an individual learns about the social order of *dharma,* but as one's own personality develops one begins to recognize his or her own particular *dharma,* or *sva dharma.* As indicated earlier, it is the *sva dharma* of Arjuna with which the *Bhagavad Gita* is concerned. Arjuna's *sva dharma* involved him in battle because of family and caste obligations, but it also involved him in a particular devotional relationship with Krishna which freed him to fight the war with a sense of detachment. Individuals cannot fulfill their *dharma* by running away from social obligations. However, a true awareness of the order of the universe comes not from the fulfillment of these duties alone but from the ability to see the higher principle of order to which those transient duties point. Because ordinary *dharma* points beyond itself to a higher order, the pursuit of *dharma* becomes a truly religious dimension of life.

Dharma is manifest in every aspect of life, yet it also points to the outer limits, or ultimate structure, of Reality. Because *dharma* is involved so closely in the ordering of ordinary life, other forms of expression are used when Indian religious thinkers want to emphasize the transcendent dimension of Reality.

Brahman

The word *Brahman* means roughly "the fullness" or "the ultimate." The concept is used in order to refer to the ultimate Reality without employing images from this world. *Brahman* is truly beyond this world, and any descriptions used to define the concept would falsify and limit it.

Part I alluded briefly to the teachings of the *Upanishads,* where some of the earliest explorations of the concept of *Brahman* took place. The Upanishadic teachers show how *Brahman* is the hidden essence underlying the cosmic forces or the Vedic gods.

The favorite channel for exploring *Brahman* in the *Upanishads,* however, is through the examination of the self, or consciousness. Consciousness, the teachers argue, is many-layered. Human beings are aware of waking consciousness, of dreamy consciousness, and even in a vague way of the quiet consciousness of deep sleep. The Upanishadic teachers then go on to argue that there is a fourth, or deeper, consciousness which is our true self—a self, or *atman,* which is identical with a universal *Atman.* This *Atman,* if truly the universal Self, can be nothing else but *Brahman* itself.

The many different gods and goddesses in Hindu religion are in some way or another manifestations of *Brahman.* The great philosopher Shankara argued that the philosophical idea of *Brahman* could only be described negatively, for in its highest form it was "without attributes"; but he saw no difficulty in also holding to a "with attributes" version of *Brahman* which would correspond to any one of the different gods which people found inspired their devotion. According to this idea, there could be a kind of continual transformation of the symbols of the divine depending upon the capability of the devotees. In an extended series, the transformation might move in this fashion:

Crude magical stones by the roadside;
> to

the anthropomorphic household, village, or caste deities with local names, rituals, and myths;
> to

temple deities such as Ganesha (elephant-headed son of Shiva), Hanuman (monkey assistant to Rama), Sarasvati (goddess of learning and wife of the creator god Brahma), Venkateshvara (boy form of Vishnu), Krishna (*avatara,* or incarnation, of Vishnu), Rama (*avatara* of Vishnu);
> to

one of the older Vedic deities such as Indra (warrior), Agni (fire), Brahma (creator), Surya (sun);
> to

the Ishvara, or Lord, of one of the three major sectarian groups of Vaishnavism (Vishnu), Shaivism (Shiva), or Shaktism (usually the goddess Kali),
> to

Brahman with attributes;
> to, finally,

Brahman without attributes.

While the devotee was absolutely committed to the particular form he or she worshiped at the time, Shankara believed that each of these forms of *Brahman* led the devotee on to higher forms, and in that sense all were proper manifestations of *Brahman.*

The question has often been asked whether the idea of God in Hinduism should be thought of as monistic, monotheistic, polytheistic, or animistic. The answer cannot be a simple and final one. Shankara's view could be described as monism—the doctrine which says that there is finally only one Reality, in this case *Brahman*, because the idea that either individuals or the world as such are separate and different from *Brahman* is really an illusion, or *maya*. But even if the central position of Shankara is monism, much of the actual religious life of India is monotheistic, for in practice most Hindus worship one God whom they consider the Lord of the Universe. Another great philosopher Ramanuja tried to argue that the world and the souls of living beings, while ultimately part of *Brahman*, were separate and distinct in the context of worship and that his worship of Vishnu was, therefore, monotheistic. The assertion that Hindus are polytheists is not really correct. Hindus do not believe in a group of gods who together share in divinity. In Hindu worship there is always one god in view, even though there is a general recognition that God takes different forms at different times. Finally, some people have stated that Indians are animistic, in that they seem to worship rivers, mountains, trees, rocks, and animals. Again, this characterization misses the point, for it is not natural objects themselves which are worshiped, but the hidden Reality which is in some way symbolized by these objects. In fact, Hindus have a transcendental idea of the divine as something radically different from the world of *samsara*, or nature; but it is precisely because the divine is so radically different that they feel free to use a variety of symbolic forms in their worship of it.

As we have seen, Hindus come to think of the divine through two rather different channels; that of *dharma* (the order which is evident in the universe) and that of *Brahman* (the ultimate Reality which radically transcends the world). The first channel reassures an individual that the cosmic and moral order have meaning and that the divine is present in the world. The second inspires the awe and devotion which makes Hinduism both profoundly mystical and richly varied in its practices.

A yoga class learns the basic position.

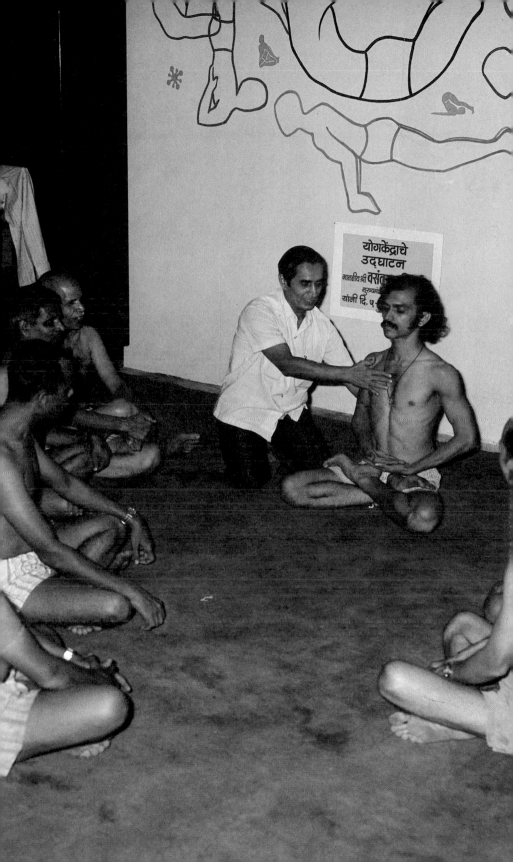

WHAT IS THE WAY TO ACHIEVE SALVATION?

Yoga

The word *yoga* is from the root meaning "to yoke"; thus *yoga* means the "harness," or discipline, which one uses to bring life into line with some goal. *Yoga* has become a familiar word even in North America, where it is usually associated with a special kind of physical exercise that originated in India. But in India the word *yoga* has a wider variety of meanings and usually refers to the rather specific discipline of the *Yoga Sutra* text or to the different paths a religious person may choose in his or her quest for salvation.

The *Yoga Sutra* of Patanjali is an old text dating from about the beginning of the Christian Era. Its philosophical starting point is the same as that found in a popular school of philosophy called Samkhya. The Samkhya school of philosophy states very clearly that there are two distinct kinds of reality: one which is consciousness and is called *purusha;* the other which is the world with all its many forms, which is called *prakriti.* Consciousness gets entangled with the world, which spins out its numerous mental and material forms as a kind of dramatic show for the sake of consciousness. Consciousness cannot just flee from the world which thus manifests itself. Its only alternative is to find a way of harnessing this experience. For many followers of Samkhya philosophy this is primarily an intellectual exercise, but for the practitioners of *yoga* it is a combination of physical and mental discipline. Beginning with the most distant and material forms and proceeding inward, the *yogi* uses exercises to gain mastery over the activity of the body, then of the breath, and finally of the mental processes. This gradual harnessing of the restless forms which make up the world eventually quiets the activity of that world and sets consciousness free from the world's distracting allure so that it can truly be itself again.

Even when it is used in other contexts, the word *yoga* continues to connote the attempt of consciousness to harness the restless activity of the world. While this concept of harnessing the restless world was understood as the general task of any path of salvation, Hinduism was always careful to see that all individuals had a pathway they could follow. Buddhism and Jainism had tended to emphasize one path *(marga),* and in reaction to that the *Bhagavad Gita* explicitly states that there are a number of paths. In an attempt to clarify the concept of "path," the *Bhagavad Gita* carefully shifts the emphasis from the Buddhist word *marga,* with its group-based connotation, to the word *yoga,* with its emphasis on the individual's own discipline. The *Bhagavad Gita* teaches that there are a number of different *yogas,* or ways of harnessing the world, and that a part of the search for salvation which each individual undertakes will involve the discovery of the *yoga* most appropriate to that individual.

The three major *yogas* suggested by the *Bhagavad Gita* are the ways of *jnana* (knowledge), *karma* (action), and *bhakti* (devotion). A *jnana yoga* would, for example, be carefully following the *Upanishads* or Shankara when they teach that the world is illusory and that the only true knowledge is to know that the self, or consciousness, is really a part of the highest Self, *Brahman/Atman.* To know *Brahman* in this sense is not to know *about* it but to have gained the mystical knowledge which makes an individual one with *Brahman.* A *karma yoga* would be a discipline similar to that which Arjuna developed as he headed into battle—a *yoga* in which a person acts according to his or her normal *dharma,* but with detachment rather than passion and with an understanding that the action is in perfect harmony with the soul of the universe. A *bhakti yoga* would be one of the many forms of devotion in which, through ritual and devotion to a chosen deity, a person becomes one with the Lord and, through him, with the highest *Brahman.*

Whatever form of discipline is used, *yoga* as a concept means that every person seeking salvation must make an effort, must recognize the need for something higher, and must pull the disorder of *samsara* together and reach out toward the goal. Hinduism more than most religions is not satisfied with the individual's mere participation in a religious group. It insists that it is only through the development of a personal *yoga* that the individual will find the way to salvation. But salvation itself is not to be confused with the *yoga,* or way. The final state is much more than that.

Moksha

The word *moksha* means "final release." It suggests a self that is entangled in *samsara* and that is finally released to be itself again. This release should not be confused with death or with the exhausted end of a busy life, for death leads only to another birth and more entanglement. Release is rather a goal achieved only after many lives and much effort, when the proper *yoga* has been found and a true oneness with *Brahman* has been realized.

Moksha is usually thought of as beyond description. The Buddhists are insistent on this point, and define *moksha* as Nirvana (nonbreath), or that which is totally other than what we know in this life. Some

Buddhists visualize the quest for Nirvana as the crossing of the sea of life, where one leaves this shore on a raft before being able to see the other shore. The Hindus share this general feeling that salvation is not something that can be described, but is rather something toward which our experience of *duhkha,* or pain, drives us and therefore something for which we long.

Hindus, however, go further than Buddhists when they point out that salvation will consist of three aspects of reality blended into a perfect unity. One of these aspects of reality is *sat* (being), another is *chit* (consciousness), and the third is *ananda* (bliss). *Sat-chit-ananda* taken together constitutes an experience of the Absolute which an individual is capable of knowing as he or she is liberated from entanglements with *samsara* and which allows the consciousness to be its true self, to again become a part of *Brahman.*

For Hindus the search for a suitable *yoga* and the longing for eventual *moksha,* or release, are the overriding ends of life. This does not mean that they do not take delight in the beauties of nature or become deeply involved in the responsibilities of society. But it does mean that life's true fulfillment always lies beyond, in the attainment of true *moksha,* or salvation.

Each of the six answers to the basic questions of Hinduism *(samsara, duhkha, dharma, Brahman, yoga,* and *moksha)* describes a different dimension of human experience in the gradual awakening which the individual undergoes as he or she comes to see the true nature of existence. But these ideas are not like doctrines which are taught in isolation and which people are asked to believe. They are rather the ideas people accumulate through stories, festivals, and ceremonies as they come to accept their tradition and as they learn to express themselves in a variety of religious practices. These practices will be considered in Part III, which follows.

A bullock is colorfully decorated in preparation for a festival celebration.

Practices

The material in this section is not found in many books on Hinduism. Writers often try to make Hinduism look as much like a Western religion as possible. They therefore select from the great mass of material only those elements which seem to be theological or philosophical in character. Then with the help of historical imagination, they attempt to string those elements together to make a tradition. As a result, the actual content of the religious life of ordinary people is often ignored.

This section describes some of the content of the religious life of the ordinary people as it is expressed in the stories, festivals, and ceremonies through which they communicate with one another in their homes and villages. Some of the stories may seem quite simple; the festivals may appear to be nothing more than unsophisticated people having a good time; and even the ceremonies may seem old-fashioned. Indians think of the stories, festivals, ceremonies, and private patterns of devotion as part of the ever-changing scene of life, and there is no single pattern that is more sacred than all others. Every family, caste, or village has its own set of stories, festivals, and ceremonies. It would be impossible to describe them all, so the authors must subjectively choose certain ones in the hope of providing some insight into Hindu religious practices. What is important to understand is the fact that all Hindus are raised on a collection of stories, a number of enjoyable festivals, and a set of carefully observed ceremonies. Underlying these stories, festivals, and ceremonies are certain attitudes toward life which slowly and imperceptibly become a part of the personality of every Hindu, and indeed most Indians.

Part III is divided into four sections. The first will present stories, the second will deal with festivals, the third will consider religious ceremonies and include a detailed description of the marriage ritual, and the fourth will deal with patterns of religious devotion.

STORIES

One of the greatest pleasures of Indian children is listening to stories. Most Indian homes are extended families, in that parents, grandparents, uncles, aunts, and cousins all live together. Indian children have many older people around to tell them stories. The immediate purpose of these stories may be to stir the emotions of children, but they also serve to teach them about the holy places of pilgrimage, great scholars, heroes or heroines, and the traditional Indian attitudes toward life. The following three stories are typical of those dear to Indian children.

The Mud Pie and the Dry Leaf

The Mud Pie and the Dry Leaf were great friends. As they were growing old they decided to make a pilgrimage to Banaras, the holy city on the banks of the Ganges River. They believed that if they washed themselves in the Ganges their sins would be erased. Being good friends, they discussed the distance they had to travel and the perils along the way. They agreed that heavy rains and gusts of wind would be the greatest hazards. So the Dry Leaf said he would cover his friend and shield him from danger if it rained, and the Mud Pie said he would do the same if there was a strong wind.

The two had gone some distance when the winds started blowing. The Mud Pie sat on his friend and saved him. A little later the rains came. Then the Dry Leaf covered his friend and saved him. The sun shone again, and the two friends resumed their journey. A few days later the clouds darkened the skies once again. Heavy rains were accompanied by strong gusts of wind. Although the friends tried their best to help each other, the Dry Leaf was blown away and the Mud Pie was washed away.

The Fable of Kanya Kumari[1]

There was a beautiful princess in this southern part of the country whose hand was sought in marriage by many valiant princes. Finally a handsome and noble prince was chosen to be the bridegroom. Great preparations were made for the wedding. The marriage feast, which consisted of many exotic dishes, was prepared by the best cooks of the land. Many different kinds of rice were cooked. The bride, bedecked with jewels, looked radiant in her lovely wedding *sari.* Everything was ready. But due to some unknown reason, the bridegroom failed to show up. Alas! Where there had been great rejoicing, there was now mourning and sadness. The great wedding feast went to waste. The remains turned into multicolored sand—sand resembling rice and sand resembling broken rice. The princess died of a broken heart soon after. Hence the place came to be called Kanya Kumari.

Panini[2]

When Panini was a young lad, an elderly man who was adept at palmistry took the boy's right hand and studied it carefully. After some time, he shook his head sadly. Panini was puzzled and asked what was wrong.

The old man said, "You are a fine lad. Your heart is sound. You have a good mind and your life line is not bad. But alas, there is absolutely nothing where a career line should be! You might end up as a nonentity and a dunce."

Panini thanked the old man for his kindness. Then he took a small knife and made a long, straight line where his career line should have been. After that he put his mind to his studies. He won great renown as a scholar, and modern scholars now look on him as the greatest of all Indian grammarians.

---

[1]Kanya Kumari (virgin princess) is the southernmost point of India. It is a sacred place and has a beautiful shore temple. Both sunrise and sunset can be seen from the same vantage point. The sand on the seashore is multicolored and of an amazing variety.

[2]Panini was a Sanskrit scholar of antiquity. The word *pani* means "hand."

The Shore Temple on the southern tip of India (Cape Comorin).

One famous collection of fables from ancient India is the *Pancha-tantra* (meaning "five parts"). It was probably compiled about 200 B.C. but contains many stories that are older. The stories in this collection were supposed to have been used by a Brahmin scholar who had to teach the three sons of a famous king. When he started teaching, he realized that the boys were not very bright. So he told these stories in order to help them learn something about how to deal with people and situations in life. It is not customary for Indians to attach morals to stories. They usually tell stories and hope the children will be inspired. In the case of the *Panchatantra*, however, a moral is tagged on to every tale. Here is one fable from this collection.

The Turtle Who Fell off a Stick

Near a certain lake there lived a turtle and two swans. They were good friends. One year there was a severe drought and the lake started to dry up. The three wondered how they could save themselves. Suddenly the turtle had a brilliant idea. He said, "First, find a lake full of water; then bring me a strong stick. I'll hold onto the middle of it by my mouth. You hold the ends and carry me to our new lake."

The birds agreed it was an excellent idea but warned him, "When we are flying, take care not to open your mouth!"

Finally the swans found the ideal lake and the stick and got ready for their flight. They had to fly over a city. People looked up in amazement and said, "Look at those clever birds carrying something. It is a turtle!"

The turtle heard this and started to say, "What is all this excitement about? Me?" Alas! He didn't and couldn't finish what he had to say.

Moral: Silence is golden.

Just as children in the West learn about historical heroes and hero-ines, Indian children come to know the heroes and heroines of Indian history. Gautama the Buddha, Ashoka, Prithvi Raj, Padmini the Rajput queen, Rani Lakshmi Bhai, Shivaji, and Mahatma Gandhi are a few of these. The following is the story of one of these great Indians.

Prithvi Raj

Prithvi Raj, a brave and handsome prince of medieval times, was in love with a beautiful princess from a nearby kingdom. In those days it was the custom for kings to hold *svayamvaras* for their daughters. (The term means "choosing a husband for oneself.")

One day the king (the father of the lovely princess) issued a royal proclamation with much fanfare, inviting all the eligible princes from far and near to assemble at his palace for his daughter's *svayamvara*. But because of a family feud, the king did not invite Prithvi Raj.

On the day of the *svayamvara* the great hall of the palace was lavishly decorated and shone with the splendor of a thousand lights. All the princes had assembled and were seated according to rank and position. The king not only had neglected to invite Prithvi Raj, but also wanted to insult him further. So he had a stuffed effigy of the prince made and ordered it to be placed near the door of the great hall, as *dvara palaka* (doorkeeper). In spite of all this, the princess, who had heard of the valor and nobility of Prithvi Raj, had fallen in love with him; and unknown to her father, she had exchanged messages with him about what was happening.

Finally the auspicious moment came when the princess would arrive and garland the suitor of her choice. Special music and the sound of drums announced that moment. The door of the inner chambers opened and the princess, in shining bridal array, slowly came forward and walked across the palace hall. Her dazzling beauty could not be hidden by her veil. People watched her movements with bated breath.

As she reached the door, she deliberately stopped and threw her fragrant garland of flowers around the neck of the ludicrous effigy of Prithvi Raj! Before the shocked and angry king and the throng of guests could think or act, in came the noble Prithvi Raj accompanied by a band of faithful warriors. He carried his beautiful bride over the threshold of her father's palace, set her on his horse, and galloped away to his kingdom.

Kalidasa, the poet-dramatist of ancient times, has often been called the Shakespeare of India. His *Shakuntala* is unrivaled in the annals of Indian literature for its romantic beauty and dramatic appeal. The story originally appeared in the first book of the *Mahabharata*, where the lineage of the chief characters is given. Kalidasa made minor changes and transformed it into a drama of great charm and literary merit.

Shakuntala

Shakuntala was a beautiful maiden born of the union between a powerful sage and the heavenly nymph Menaka. She was adopted by the kindly sage Kanva and grew up in his *ashrama* (hermitage) in the forest in the company of two *sakhis* (girl friends). They spent their time watering the jasmine plants, playing with the pet fawns of the hermitage, and helping the nursemaid with household duties.

One day the king of the land, Dushyanta, was hunting in the forest. By mistake he chased one of the pet fawns of the hermitage. Realizing his error, he came in haste to apologize to the sage. Kanva was away at the time but, seeing the lovely Shakuntala, Dushyanta fell in love with her. At the request of some of the hermits of the place, Dushyanta stayed at the hermitage to rid them of the forest demons who terrorized the area.

As the days passed, Shakuntala fell in love with the royal guest. Being too shy to make her love known, she wrote about her feelings on a lotus leaf using her nails; her *sakhis* teasingly offered to take the leaf to the king. But Dushyanta, who had overhead their conversation, came forward, claimed the unique love letter, and declared his love for Shakuntala. They got married, as forest people do, by a simple exchange of garlands. Their happiness of a few days was cut short when messengers arrived requesting the king to return to his kingdom, since urgent matters of state required his presence there. Both Shakuntala and Dushyanta were dismayed at the thought of parting. Dushyanta consoled the tearful Shakuntala and promised to send a suitable retinue to escort her to their palace. He put his royal signet ring on her finger, warning her never to part with it.

After Dushyanta's departure, Shakuntala was lonely and listless. One day she was sitting on the doorstep of the hermitage thinking about her absent husband. She did not see the sage Durvasa approaching. Durvasa was well known for his quick temper and devastating curses; people were usually careful not to annoy him in any manner.

Seeing that Shakuntala did not get up to greet him, Durvasa flew into a rage. He shook his fist and shouted at poor Shakuntala, "This is insufferable! You! You have forgotten your duty to a guest. Therefore the one you are thinking of will also forget you!"

Shakuntala's *sakhis* fell on their knees and pleaded with the sage to forgive the gentle Shakuntala and lift the curse from her.

Durvasa, his anger abating somewhat, said, "I cannot take back my curse! Maybe I will soften it a little bit. The person she was thinking of will remember Shakuntala when he sees an object he has given her."

Indian children, like these attending a day-care center near Poona, delight in listening to traditional stories.

When the sage Kanva returned to the hermitage, he was happy to learn that Shakuntala had married a man worthy of her. He also heard a heavenly voice saying that the son she was expecting would one day become a great emperor. The sage, however, felt that Shakuntala should be with her husband. So preparations were made to send Shakuntala to Dushyanta. The womenfolk were worried because Shakuntala did not have clothes suitable for a queen. But Kanva's meditation was so powerful that beautiful clothes and glittering ornaments appeared on the branches of a tree to which he pointed. Clothed in regal attire, Shakuntala looked radiant as she knelt to receive the sage's blessings. Her nursemaid and a few hermits accompanied her on her journey to Dushyanta's palace.

On the way she stopped to bathe in the holy river. Unknown to Shakuntala, the signet ring slipped off her finger and was carried away by the swift-flowing waters of the river.

In the meantime, Durvasa's curse had gone to work, and King Dushyanta forgot all about Shakuntala. On their arrival at the palace, Shakuntala and her companions were ushered into Dushyanta's presence. His courtiers were standing around. The hermits told the king of the prediction sage Kanva had heard about his future son. Dushyanta thought this was some kind of joke. The old nursemaid was dumbfounded. She asked Shakuntala to lift her veil.

Still Dushyanta did not recognize her. In utter bewilderment he said, "She is indeed most beautiful! But I have never before set eyes on her!"

The nursemaid and the hermits, distressed though they were, could not take Shakuntala back with them. The rejected wife started to stumble out of the palace when the court priest, a kindly old man, rose from his seat. He said he would take Shakuntala home and his wife would look after her until her baby was born. As they were leaving, Shakuntala's mother, the nymph Menaka, appeared and snatched her daughter away into the clouds. Later Menaka was to leave her daughter in the care of another old sage.

A few days later a fisherman was caught in the marketplace trying to sell the king's signet ring. He was beaten up by angry soldiers as he protested his innocence and was dragged unceremoniously into the king's presence. As he knelt before the king, he repeated that he had not stolen the ring but had found it in the belly of a fish he had caught that morning.

Memories came flooding back to Dushyanta. Now he remembered his wife! He could not forgive himself for his cruelty to Shakuntala. After rewarding the fisherman amply, Dushyanta sent for the court priest so he could get Shakuntala back; but he was told that a heavenly nymph had taken her away into the clouds and she had vanished.

A few years passed. Dushyanta was inconsolable. One day he was invited by Indra to help the gods in their battle against the demons.

After the enemies were vanquished, Dushyanta returned to earth. By chance he came upon a peaceful hermitage where he saw a handsome little boy wrestling with a lion's cub. As the boy played, his amulet (a charm bracelet) fell off his arm. Dushyanta picked it up and gave it to the boy. Some women of the hermitage who were standing nearby were amazed! The amulet had been put on the child's arm by the old sage of the hermitage. If any man other than the boy's father touched it, it would turn into a snake and bite him. Seeing that Dushyanta was not harmed, the women excitedly ran in to call Shakuntala. The child, named Bharata, was indeed Dushyanta's son. Shakuntala came out and it was a most happy reunion. Dushyanta knelt in front of Shakuntala and asked her forgiveness.

The sage blessed the couple and their son as they were leaving to go back to Dushyanta's kingdom. Exhorting the king to always work hard for the happiness and well-being of his people, he said, "Bharata will become a great emperor one day, and our country will be named Bharat[3] after him."

The following story is included to convey some idea of what is meant by *bhakti,* or devotion.

Sudaman

Sudaman was as poor as the proverbial church mouse. He and his wife were virtuous people and bore their poverty with dignity and calm. Sudaman had one ambition in life, which was to see Krishna, the Lord of the Universe. After much planning and very little preparation, he started one morning on the trip to see Lord Krishna. On one end of his *dhoti,* or waist cloth, he had a handful of rice tied as in a pouch—an offering he was taking to his lord. Sudaman and his wife had starved for many days so that they could save that much rice. Sudaman's wife had cleaned it and polished it so that each grain glistened like a tiny elongated pearl.

After many days of walking, Sudaman finally reached the abode of Lord Krishna. His feet were aching. His clothes were dirty. But as he stood behind the throng of people and strained his neck to catch a glimpse of Lord Krishna, a strange thing happened. The Lord rose

---

[3]India's postage stamps have "Bharat," the traditional name, written in Sanskrit near the name "India" written in English.

from his seat, walked through the crowd, and approached Sudaman. He took him by the hand, saying, "My friend Sudaman, I've been waiting all this time for your arrival! Come and have a seat with me."

As Sudaman sat, dumb with amazement, Krishna spoke again. "And now my friend, what have you brought for me?"

Sudaman was most embarrassed and would not answer. How could he give a handful of rice to the Lord of the Universe? But Krishna took hold of the pouch and untied it. Everybody was dazzled by what they saw. Where there had been a handful of rice, there was more than a handful of gold!

Krishna said, "You have brought me the finest gift anyone ever gave me. Now go back in peace, and may you and your wife have joy and comfort for the rest of your lives."

The story of Prahlad deals with Nara-Simha (half man, half lion), one of the ten *avataras*, or incarnations, of Lord Vishnu.

Prahlad

Prahlad was the son of a wicked *asura* (demon) king. *Asuras* were the sworn enemies of the *devas* (gods), and delighted in leading lives of *adharma* (lack of virtue) and in tormenting humanity.

Prahlad, however, due to some extraordinary circumstances early in his childhood, had come under the influence of the sage Narada, who had shown the young child the path of *dharma*. Narada had also taught the lad to be a devotee of Vishnu.

When Prahlad's father heard him sing hymns in praise of Vishnu, he became enraged. He engaged special tutors for Prahlad so they could teach the boy the way of the *asuras*. Their teaching, however, was of no avail. Prahlad still continued to be a devotee of Vishnu.

One day the king heard Prahlad again singing the praises of Vishnu. "Where is this Vishnu?" he thundered.

Prahlad calmly answered his father, "He is everywhere, my sire!"

The king pointed to a huge pillar, shouting, "If he is everywhere, he must be in that pillar too."

"Yes, my Lord!" answered Prahlad.

"We will see!" stormed his father. "I am going to crack that pillar. If I don't see your Vishnu there, I will cut off your head." And with a

Nara-Simha, one of the avataras of Lord Vishnu.

mighty heave of his sword, the giant *asura* king struck at the immense pillar.

Lo, and behold! As the pillar cracked, out came Vishnu as Nara-Simha and saved Prahlad from his wicked father. The *asura* king was dethroned, and in being destroyed by Vishnu he found his salvation. Prahlad, who was installed as king in his father's place, ruled his kingdom wisely and well.

Tales from the Ramayana

Of the ten *avataras* of Vishnu, Rama is the seventh. He is the hero of the *Ramayana*. That epic and its counterpart the *Mahabharata* contain the most widely known stories in India. The ideals set by the heroes and heroines of these stories help people to lead a life of *dharma*. The following are two episodes from the *Ramayana*.

The *Ramayana* tells how Rama, crown prince of Ayodhya and son of King Dasharatha, is banished to the forest for fourteen years. After Rama, his lovely wife Sita, and his faithful brother Lakshmana leave for the forest, King Dasharatha is grief-stricken and refuses to be consoled. The whole city of Ayodhya is plunged in sorrow. Queen Kausalya, the mother of Rama, is heartbroken and weeps by her husband's side. Just before he dies, the king reveals the following story to his wife.

SHRAVANA

When he was a young prince, Dasharatha was very fond of hunting and was an excellent marksman. His marksmanship was so good that even when he heard the sound of an animal in the distance and in the dark, he could send an arrow in the direction of the sound and kill the animal.

One evening, feeling very restless, Dasharatha went hunting. It was after dusk, and darkness had filled the forest. Before long he heard a noise, as though an elephant were drawing water with its trunk. He took aim and sent a swift arrow hissing through the forest like an enraged cobra.

Moments later, he heard a voice crying out in pain. "O God! I am stricken! Who would want to kill me? I am a poor hermit boy and have never hurt anyone in my life!"

Dasharatha trembled with an unknown fear. He stumbled in the direction of the voice and came to the riverbank. There, lying in a pool of blood, was Shravana, a young hermit, with a half-filled pitcher of water by his side.

The boy spoke again. "O! Why did you commit this heinous sin? I was innocently filling the pitcher when your arrow struck me. My parents are old and blind! Who will look after them now? Fill this pitcher with water and take it to my parents and beg their forgiveness. If they curse you, you will be reduced to ashes. Now, please pull out the arrow. The pain is more than I can bear!"

Like a man in a dream Dasharatha obeyed the boy and pulled out the arrow. Shravana drew his last breath and lay lifeless on the riverbank.

Dasharatha filled the pitcher with water and took it to the boy's parents. Hearing footsteps they called out, "Son, why did you take so long? We were getting worried about you."

Dasharatha leaned down, touched the parents' feet,[4] and murmured, "Holy mother and father, forgive me! I am not your son but an unfortunate prince who, due to the unhappy will of fate, accidentally killed your son. I am at your mercy. Do with me as you will!"

Shravana's mother fainted.

The father spoke. "Your sin is great indeed. Because it was unwittingly done, we will not curse you and reduce you to ashes. One thing is certain. A day will come when you will suffer the pangs of separation from your beloved son, and you too will die of grief."

At their request Dasharatha led the old couple to the place where their son lay. They felt his body all over and clasped him to their bosoms. Dasharatha prepared the funeral pyre and lifted the body gently onto it. The holy couple performed the last rites and they themselves climbed and entered the funeral pyre; and thus in death they were united with their son.

The following is the most famous of all the episodes in the *Ramayana*. The whole epic picks up momentum from this dramatic point onward until it finally reaches the climax when Ravana, the demon king, is killed, Sita is rescued, and Rama's coronation with the lovely Sita by his side takes place in Ayodhya with great pomp and pageantry.

THE ABDUCTION OF SITA

The fourteen years of exile were almost over. After wandering from hermitage to hermitage, ridding the sages and their dependents of the many demons who tormented them, Rama and Sita and Lakshmana had spent the last two or three years in an idyllic place in the forest,

---

[4]In India, touching the feet is a sign of reverence and respect, particularly shown to parents, grandparents, and teachers.

not far from the banks of the river Godavari. Lakshmana, who had been tutored in practical arts, built a beautiful home where the three of them lived.

Sita's devotion to Rama was such that, though she was a delicate princess, she braved all the dangers and hardships of forest life to be with her lord. Rama's love for her was such that he was always ready to satisfy her slightest whim. Lakshmana's devotion to both Rama and Sita is proverbial, for he lived with the sole aim of serving his brother and his brother's wife, whom he revered as a mother.

One day, their peaceful life in the forest was disturbed when an ugly female demon called Shurpanaka arrived. She was none other than the sister of the dreaded Ravana, most powerful of all the demon kings. Shurpanaka was smitten by Rama's handsome and princely mien, and made unseemly advances. Rama tried to be polite as he repulsed her, but when Shurpanaka tried to hurt the lovely Sita, Lakshmana swiftly cut off her ears and nose. Howling with rage and pain, she appealed to all the demons of the forest to come to her aid. They came with their armies but were cut down by the valiant Rama and Lakshmana.

Finally Shurpanaka hastened to Ravana in Lanka and, distorting the actual facts, told him that Rama and Lakshmana had insulted and mutilated her without cause and that he, Ravana, should avenge her. She pointedly mentioned that Sita, Rama's wife, was most beautiful. Ravana gleefully devised a plan whereby he could destroy Rama and abduct Sita. Ravana's own beautiful wife as well as some of his counselors tried to dissuade him from such a heinous venture. But he would not listen.

Ravana decided to employ a ruse. He enlisted the services of a demon who turned himself into a golden deer and started prancing around the abode of Rama, who was seated with Sita by his side. Lakshmana was at the door. Seeing the beautiful deer, Sita begged Rama to capture it so she could make a pet of it. Rama was uneasy; but since he wanted to make Sita happy, he took his bow and arrows, warned Lakshmana not to leave Sita's side, and started chasing the golden deer.

The deer was a most tantalizing creature. Just when Rama thought he had it, it would elude his grasp and dart away. This game went on too long and Rama, in frustration, shot an arrow at the deer.

This rubbing from a bas-relief depicts a scene from the Ramayana.

As the deer was dying it assumed the shape of the demon and cried out, imitating Rama's voice, "O Sita! O Lakshmana! Help! Help!"

Hearing what she thought was Rama's voice, Sita told Lakshmana to hasten to help Rama. Lakshmana told her it could be a trap and that he should not leave her side. But Sita insisted so angrily that poor Lakshmana was hurt and went to look for Rama.

After Lakshmana left, Sita was startled to see a shadow darkening the door. Looking up she saw a tall, stately-looking man with a begging bowl in his hand. Thinking it was a hermit, she bowed her head and approached him to give him alms.

At this, Ravana (it was none other) threw off his disguise and, assuming his own awesome form, told Sita to give up thoughts of Rama and go with him to be his queen in Lanka.

Sita cried out that she was the faithful wife of the brave and noble Prince Rama. But turning a deaf ear to her entreaties, Ravana carried her off in his winged chariot.

Sita begged every creature she saw on the way to come to her aid. The king of the birds, Jatayu, an aged eagle of gigantic proportions, heard Sita's cry. Feeble though he was, he put up a brave fight. But his wings were cut off by the wicked Ravana, and the noble Jatayu was left bleeding and dying.

Meanwhile, when Rama saw Lakshmana, he felt a chill in his heart. He feared the worst as he and Lakshmana hastened home. Alas! Sita his beloved, the light of his home, was gone. They saw signs of the struggle and started searching the forest. They saw the animals shedding tears and soon came upon Jatayu, who with his last breath told them the awful truth of the abduction of the lovely Sita—how she was wringing her hands and crying pitifully, pleading with the dreaded demon king to release her.

Rama was filled with pain as he thought of his beloved wife. He swore he would not rest till he found Ravana and destroyed this most despicable demon, the wicked enemy of all who followed the path of *dharma.*

Shiva is usually worshiped as the awesome god of power. His benign and compassionate aspect is not often emphasized. Unlike Vishnu, who appears periodically as an *avatara,* or incarnation, Shiva is known only by his manifestations. The name Shiva literally means "the auspicious one" or "the god of grace."

The following legend should be prefaced by a brief explanation of an Indian custom. A wife in the eighth month of her first pregnancy is escorted to her parents' home where she is pampered with the delicacies of her choice. After the baby is born, the mother gets plenty of rest and nourishing food, and she and her newborn receive much attention from relatives and friends. About two months after birth, the baby and its parents go back to their own home amid much fanfare and rejoicing.

The Compassionate Lord Shiva

In this legend an expectant mother is trying to reach her parents' home. Her parents, who were to meet her on the way, are unexpectedly delayed. So the woman has to cross the waters of a flooding river alone. In her distress she calls upon the Lord Shiva to come to her aid. Lord Shiva appears as her own mother, helps her across the river, and, as the birth pangs had already begun, helps her with the delivery. He comforts her and escorts her and the baby safely to her parents' home.

The main sanctuary of the Golden Rock Temple, about two hundred miles southwest of Madras, is dedicated to Lord Shiva. Its name means "the lord who even took the form of a mother." The shrine is very popular with expectant parents, who offer oblations and prayers to the lord who was so compassionate.

FESTIVALS

There are all kinds of festivals in India. Some usher in a new season and others the New Year. Some are in celebration of the harvest season, which has great significance in India where the majority of people are dependent on the land for sustenance. As festivals are observed according to the lunar and solar calendars, there is no single New Year's Day. The New Year is ushered in at different times in different places in India. Some festivals are in honor of gods or goddesses and others re-create the atmosphere of favorite stories from the *Mahabharata* or the *Ramayana*.

Holi

The Holi festival, which ushers in the spring (in March), is well known to tourists visiting India. It is celebrated primarily in the north and is associated with Kama, the god of love. It might remind a Westerner of a Mardi Gras or Halloween celebration; people throw colored water at each other and play practical jokes.

Kumbha Mela

There is a very special religious festival called Kumbha Mela. It is considered the world's greatest religious concourse and is held about every twelve years at four sacred places in northern India. The one at the city of Allahabad is the largest, with as many as ten million pilgrims assembling from all parts of the subcontinent. A cross section of Hindu India can be seen here—peasants, merchants, paupers, misers, moneylenders, pundits and illiterates, naked holy men and the sophisticated elite. Kumbha Mela is celebrated when the sun and the moon are in Mesha (Aries) and Jupiter passes through Kumbha (Aquarius).

The Kumbha Mela is primarily a ritual bathing festival associated with Mother Ganga, or the holy river Ganges. Water from any part of the Ganges is considered sacred, but the stretch of river at Allahabad, where the Ganges and Jumna rivers join, is considered the most sacred.

Divali

Divali (or Dipavali) literally means "a garland of lights." It is considered the national festival of India since it is the most widely celebrated. This is a time when the darkness of misery and poverty is replaced by the radiance of innumerable lights. People don festive clothes. Sweets, usually made of thickened milk and sugar or with freshly grated coconut and sugar, are made and distributed lavishly. People in the wealthy mercantile communities of western India paint their houses, open new account books, start everything afresh. They pay homage to household deities, especially to Lakshmi, the goddess of wealth and good fortune.

This festival falls in the month of Kartik (October-November) and marks the beginning of the New Year for many. As the title implies, it is, above all, a festival of lights. After supper people go out to view the rows and rows of lights illuminating every household—tiny earthenware lamps with saucerlike depressions holding the oil and the wicks. The lamps burn throughout the night. It is a beautiful sight that defies description.

Worshipers bathing in the Ganges River.

Fireworks are set off, to the great delight of children for whom Divali is, perhaps, the most joyous of all festivals. In Bengal, Divali illuminations take the form of lighted torches on long poles. Some believe that the torches serve as guiding lights for the souls of visiting departed ancestors.

The exact origin of Divali, like that of many Indian festivals, is shrouded in antiquity. Vaishnavites (those who worship Vishnu as the supreme deity) believe that Divali grew out of the magnificent celebrations connected with the coronation of Rama as the king of Ayodhya. According to the *Ramayana,* Sita, the beautiful wife of Rama, is rescued and enthroned beside him. She looks radiant in shining garments and jewelry. There is great rejoicing in Ayodhya, for the demon of darkness has been removed. The streets and houses of Ayodhya shine with the radiance of rows of lights. People who had been sorrowing long in the absence of their rightful king have donned their brightest clothing and celebrate by throwing flower petals in the air as symbols of gladness. Thus many look upon Divali as a colorful and joyful festival celebrating the happy ending of the epic *Ramayana.*

Onam

Divali is little celebrated in Kerala, chiefly because the Onam festival occurs there a few weeks earlier. (Celebrations are usually a drain on the family purse, and people are unable to indulge in them too often.) The Onam festival takes place early in the month of September in the midst of the harvest season. The torrential monsoons have stopped, and the crops are abundant. People wear and exchange new clothes, usually made of fine cotton with gold borders. Houses are cleaned and decorated. The prayer rooms are profusely decorated with flower petals, while courtyards are adorned with complicated geometrical designs made with rice flour mixed with water.

All sorts of vegetables grow in Kerala. Elaborate vegetarian dishes and different kinds of rice and yogurt preparations are served at the Onam feast. Bananas are a must for this festival. Different varieties of plantains are grown in Kerala, but only one is called the banana. It is much bigger than the other plantains, has a different texture, and is rich in protein.

Women, their coiled hair decked with jasmine and roses, dance special Onam dances. Men indulge in vigorous sports. The famous boat race of Kerala is held at this time.

The festival is said to have originated as follows:

An *asura* (demon) king named Mahabali ruled in southern India (probably over what is now Tamil Nadu and Kerala). Unlike the typical *asura,* Mahabali followed the path of *dharma* and ruled over his people wisely and well. They in turn adored him. Under Mahabali's rule there was no shortage of any good thing; there was no theft or murder, neither famine nor pestilence, and all were equal.

The gods soon became jealous of Mahabali's popularity. They held council together and decided to send Vishnu to earth as Vamana, a mean and hungry-looking dwarf. Vamana approached Mahabali and asked of him a bit of land, as much as he could measure in three strides. Mahabali, noting Vamana's diminutive size, said he would be most happy to give him the land. At this, before the amazed eyes of on-lookers, Vamana grew into a giant of immense proportions. He measured the whole of the earth in two strides and then asked Mahabali where he could place his foot for the third stride. Mahabali, recognizing Lord Vishnu, knelt in front of him and requested that the god place his foot on his head. Vamana stepped on Mahabali and pushed him down to the nether world.

Before he was banished thus, Mahabali asked for a favor—that he be allowed to visit his beloved people once a year. Vishnu granted his wish. The people of Kerala believe that Mahabali visits them at Onam time. Everybody tries to be joyous and happy so that when Mahabali comes he will be pleased.

Festival Deities

The following deities are especially celebrated in festivals.

Lakshmi, the consort of Vishnu, is worshiped widely as the goddess of beauty, wealth, and prosperity. The wife in the home is compared to Lakshmi—the symbol of light, prosperity, and good fortune. Although Kubera is the god of wealth and his fabled celestial abode sparkles with jewels, he is not considered worthy of worship because he is selfish, miserly, and interested only in amassing riches for himself.

Durga and Kali are worshiped widely, especially in Bengal. They are considered manifestations of Parvati (the consort of Shiva), who is the mother goddess—the symbol of strength and power. Durga is represented as having a gentle face and eight arms, each of which holds a weapon. Kali, on the other hand, is formidable and is represented as black and wearing a garland of skulls. She is said to have destroyed *kala* (time) itself.

Sarasvati, the consort of Brahma the creator, is the goddess of learning—the patroness of all the creative arts and sciences. She is represented as reclining on a swan or peacock with a *vina* (a type of musical instrument) in her hand. During Sarasvati Puja,[5] a festival in her honor, scholars, musicians, and artists all worship her. Books, pens, musical instruments, paintbrushes, paints, sculptor's tools—all of these are placed in front of her image for a day. Hindu school boys and girls eagerly look forward to this day of relaxation and recess from schoolwork.

Ganesha (or Ganapati), the son of Shiva, is the god who removes all obstacles. Hence his aid is invoked at the beginning of any important venture in life. Ganapati Puja is the most important of all festivals in Maharashtra.

Hanuman, the monkey god, is worshiped widely, especially in Gujarat, because of his devotion to Rama. His relentless efforts to find Sita and his superhuman acts of heroism make him a great favorite of all devotees of Lord Rama.

RELIGIOUS CEREMONIES

The reader may be aware by now that Hinduism is a way of life as well as a religion. Whether he or she meditates on *Brahman* the Absolute or worships one deity or many deities, every Hindu is expected by tradition to follow the path of *dharma,* or duty. It is considered the *dharma* of every individual to be initiated through religious rites *(samskaras)* into successive stages of life. There are many *samskaras* in the life of an individual—one when a baby is born, one when an infant is named (usually ten days after birth), one when a child is given his or her first haircut at about the age of one year, another when a boy is consecrated or initiated (usually between the ages of five and twelve). Then comes the marriage ceremony and, finally, ceremonies associated with death[6] and with the paying of homage to ancestral souls on the anniversaries of their death.

---

[5]*Puja* means "worship" or "homage."

[6]Many Hindus keep the water of the holy river Ganges in their homes so that it can be administered to the dying. Many go on pilgrimages to holy places as they near the end of their lives, since it is hoped that by dying in a holy place such as Banaras one can attain *moksha.* According to Hindu custom, the body of the deceased must be cremated.

This boy is undergoing the rite of thread investiture, one of the most important samskaras in a Hindu's religious life.

Of the four stages in a man's life, that of a *grihastha* (householder) is usually considered the most important. The wife is known as *sahadharmini,* or "co-worker in doing *dharma."* The husband and wife are jointly called *dampatis,* or "joint owners of the household."

The lawgiver Manu is often maligned as having assigned an inferior position to women. An oft-quoted passage of his reads: "Her father protects her in childhood, her husband protects her in youth, her sons protect her in old age. A woman does not deserve independence." Many have interpreted this passage to mean that women have no freedom. However, a different perspective may be seen in another quotation from Manu: "Where women verily are honored there the gods rejoice; where however they are not honored there all sacred rights prove fruitless. . . . Regarding this as the highest *dharma* of all four classes, husbands though weak must strive to protect their wives. . . . [Women] are deserving worship, [are] the resplendent lights of homes and divinities of good luck."

A story is told of two *rajas* (kings) of southern India playing for the chess championship. The game went on for hours. The wife of the host was in the same room rocking the baby's cradle and singing a lullaby. Seeing her husband about to make the wrong move, she quickly gave him the winning clue, working it into the words of the lullaby. The situation was saved. Her husband won the game and the title.

This story gives some insight into the nature of the husband-wife relationship. The Indian word for creator, teacher, sword, mountain, and protector are masculine. The words for strength, power, salvation, and intelligence are feminine.

Marriage

Kanyadana (gift of the maiden) is prescribed by the *dharma shastras* (sacred texts). It is the duty of parents to find a suitable husband for their daughter of marriageable age, between eighteen and twenty-one usually. When parents settle on a suitable partner, the horoscopes of the intended couple are matched and the marriage ceremony is scheduled for a favorable day at the favorable time. This custom of arranged marriages may seem strange to the Westerner. But since parents have the welfare of their children at heart and go to endless trouble to find suitable partners, such marriages more often than not turn out to be happy and successful. Marriage quite often is just the beginning of a love-*dharma* relationship for the newlyweds. Even in cases where young people find each other and fall in love, the marriage between them must be formally arranged by the parents.

Marriage is an occasion for great rejoicing and lavish entertaining. Quite often, the guests will be requested to come with their families and friends.

The guests are greeted at the entrance of the wedding hall by the relatives of the bride or groom (depending on who has extended the invitation). Rose water is sprinkled on them as they enter the hall, and beautiful maidens in festive *saris* offer flowers and sandalwood paste; at the conclusion of the ceremony the flowers are thrown at the bride and groom as a symbol of blessing. The guests are seated in the hall and solemnly await the commencement of the marriage ceremony. It is conducted on a four-cornered raised platform with wooden pillars and a decorative roof. This pavilion, or *mandapa,* resembles an old-fashioned chariot without wheels and is decorated with cloth of red, white, and gold. If the people are wealthy, the marriage *mandapa* is completely covered with jasmine and rose petals.

The ceremony itself is the crucial part of the wedding. Since the ceremony is not a contract but a *samskara* (religious rite), the bride and groom, who are seated side by side, exchange no vows. Instead, whatever be the caste or *jati* of the couple, the Brahmin priests who are officiating at the wedding chant *mantras* from sacred texts invoking the gods to bless the sacred union. A lighted lamp with five or seven[7] wicks symbolizes Agni—the celestial and domestic god of fire—who is invoked as the chief and divine *sakshin* (witness) of the sacred ceremony. The auspicious moment is usually announced by special music and the sound of drums. At that moment, according to the custom in certain parts of India, a sacred thread will join the hands of the bride and groom. In the south, the sacred thread is called a *thali* and is tied around the neck of the bride by the groom at the favorable time.[8] The thread is strung with a gold grain, a tiny gold lamp, and other symbols of prosperity, good fortune, and fertility to show that the bride enters the home as the goddess Lakshmi. As soon as the *thali* is tied, the close relatives of the bride who were standing behind her will move aside, and the close relatives of the bridegroom will take their place, signifying that the bride is part of their family from that moment onward. *Saptapadi,* or taking seven steps hand-in-hand around the *mandapa,* confirms and concludes the wedding ceremony. From that moment onward the couple are "friends" for life.

Since the usual custom is for land to remain in the same family from generation to generation, the bride was formerly given a dowry

---

[7]These are considered lucky numbers.
[8]The thread is replaced by a gold chain after the ceremony.

(*stridhanam,* meaning "wealth of the woman") of money and jewelry. As that custom was sometimes abused when parents of the groom tried to extract money from parents of the bride, the system of dowry giving has been legally abolished and gifts have taken the place of the dowry. It is amazing how substantial these gifts can be in wealthy families!

The festivities begin when the wedding ceremony is over. The marriage feasts are very elaborate, and delicacies of different kinds are served on a lavish scale to guests. In the evening, if the families can afford it, there will be entertainment. Quite often Indian music and dances will be featured.

Music and Dance

In most of the festivals and ceremonies of India, music and dance play an important part. Music is used to express the tone or mood of a festival or ceremony. Different *ragas*[9] reflect the moods of joy, sadness, or excitement. In ceremonies or in dramas, which are so often part of a festival, it is the character of the music which establishes the mood of the participants. Many Westerners who have come to appreciate Indian music may not be aware that much of its richness comes from the close way in which the music reflects the cycle or aspect of life it depicts.

Dance in India is not a social phenomenon but is usually a highly developed and sophisticated form of religious art. There is a rich variety: the joyful folk dances of the tribal people, the complex dramatic dances of religious festivals (*Kathakali* of Kerala being the best known), and the sophisticated abstract expression of *bharata natyam* (dance of India). One of the best known of the *bharata natyam* dances is the one which attempts to portray the ten *avataras* (incarnations) of Vishnu. The dances, while depicting religious themes, also portray the basic emotions of human experience through subtle movement of the dancer's body and by facial expressions. The most important forms of expression are those made with various movements and placements of the hands.

---

[9]Ragas are traditional melodic patterns.

Hindu weddings are festive occasions, sometimes lasting two or three days.

PATTERNS OF WORSHIP

Any discussion of the religious life of India must include the way Hindus worship. As religion is an intensely personal matter, there are many ways in which Hindus worship the deity of their choice. Some individuals go to temples daily, some less often; others go only on special occasions—holy days or festival days. Some seek special blessings and hence go when the need is felt. Whatever the occasion, everyone takes an offering to the deity—flowers, coconuts, ghee (clarified butter), sweets, and so forth. The priest will place the offering in front of the deity, then return part of it to the devotee. If the portions are plentiful and considered delectable, the devotee will distribute them to members of the family as well as to friends and relatives. The offering thus distributed is called *prasada,* which means it has the blessing of the deity.

People also go to temples to hear discourses. These usually occur in the early evening, and a *pundit* (learned man) will expound the scriptures to the usually predominantly female audience. Because the climate is warm, these religious discourses are often held in the temple grounds. Some of the texts expounded will be in Sanskrit, some in the local language. The people who attend will mostly be simple folk. Some will listen with earnest attention while others, weary from the day's hard labor, will lean against the wall and doze. Passages from the *Bhagavad Gita* and Shankara's teachings are favored by the *pundits.* The people particularly enjoy passages written by the saints of their region.

Devotional passages such as these are often chosen:

> *Worship the Lord, you fool! When the appointed time comes, repeating the fine rules of grammar will not avail you any.* (From Shankara's hymn "Bhaja Govindam.")
>
> *The letter A is the beginning of the alphabet; even so God is the first Cause of the world. Of what use is great learning if one does not worship Him who is possessed of pure Knowledge?* (The opening lines of *Thirukkural.*[10])

The temple teaching is as much about right living as it is about devotion. Verses from the *dharma shastras* (sacred texts) are used in some parts of India. In Madras, verses from the *Thirukkural* are very popular:

> *Those who desire the higher pleasures of heaven will not act unjustly through desire of the trifling joy of this life.*

---

[10]*Thirukkural* is the "divine verse" of a Tamil saint of the second century B.C.

To bear with those who revile us even as the earth bears up with those who dig it is the first of virtues.

Forget anger toward everyone, as fountains of evil come from it.

Popular as temple worship may be, worship in the home is even more widely practiced. In most homes the prayer room is elaborately decorated and furnished with images of favorite deities on a raised dais. Pictures of gods and goddesses adorn the walls. (Even in humble homes the best wall is reserved for pictures of deities.) Five- or seven-wick oil lamps made of silver or brass are lighted at the time of prayer. Aside from morning worship, a simple *sandhya namaskaram* (dusk worship) is held.

The woman of the house is the one who is diligent about the prayer ceremony, although the householder usually takes a brief moment or two to pay homage before he leaves for work. The entire family participates in the prayer ceremony of special occasions—holy days, festival days, birthdays, anniversaries of deaths, at the start of a journey, on safe arrival from a distant land, when embarking on a special venture, after the wedding when the bride leaves the home with the groom, and so forth.

It is in these domestic ceremonies that much of the Hindu's religious life shows itself. Indeed, one can learn a great deal about Hinduism from books, but if one wishes to experience the religiousness of the Hindus, one must visit their homes.

Bibliography

Basham, Arthur L. *The Wonder That Was India: A Survey of the History and Culture of the Indian Sub-continent before the Coming of the Muslims.* New York: Taplinger, 1968.

The Bhagavad Gita. There are many editions, but the Penguin edition is inexpensive and well done.

De Bary, William T., ed. *Sources of Indian Tradition.* NewYork: Columbia University Press, 1958. This is a well-edited collection of sources.

Hopkins, Thomas. *The Hindu Religious Tradition.* Encino, Calif.: Dickenson, 1971. Easily available and worthwhile.

Markandaya, Kamala. *Nectar in a Sieve.* New York: John Day, 1955. A social novel for young people.

Rao, Raja. *The Serpent and the Rope.* New York: Pantheon, 1960. A philosophical novel.

Younger, Paul. *Introduction to Indian Religious Thought.* Philadelphia: Westminster, 1972.

Glossary

adharma. Unrighteousness; see *dharma.*

Agni. The god of fire. In the *Rig Veda,* more hymns are addressed to him than to any other god.

Akbar. Sixteenth-century Muslim emperor of the Mogul dynasty. Akbar tried to reconcile Islam and Hinduism.

ananda (lit. "bliss"). Along with *sat* and *chit* it is one of the three aspects of the state of final release.

animism. The religious belief that rocks, trees, and other natural objects have souls or spirits; in some cases, these spirits are worshipped.

Arjuna. The third of the Pandava brothers, the heroes of the *Mahabharata* epic. In the section of the *Mahabharata* known as the *Bhagavad Gita,* Arjuna, as he is about to go into battle, is taught by the Lord Krishna, who appears as his friend and charioteer.

Ashoka. A Buddhist king of the Maurya dynasty (third century B C). Ashoka conquered an empire covering most of the Indian subcontinent. He is considered the greatest king of India.

ashrama. A forest hermitage set up for meditation.

asura. A demon. In the *Rig Veda, asuras* are the enemies of the gods. They are different from *rakshasas,* who are enemies of men.

atman. Soul or self. *Atman* can refer either to the individual soul or to the soul of the Universal Reality *(Brahman).*

Aurangzeb. Eighteenth-century Muslim emperor of the Mogul dynasty. He persecuted Hindus during his reign.

avatara (lit. "descenders"). In particular, an *avatara* is the form the god Vishnu takes when he descends to the world in a time of crisis. Some of the *avataras* of Vishnu are Varaha, Vanama, Nara-Simha, Rama, and Krishna.

Ayodhya. One of the holy cities of Hinduism. Ayodhya was the capital of King Rama, the hero of the *Ramayana* epic.

Banaras. One of the holy cites of Hinduism, on the banks of the Ganges River.

Bhagavad Gita (lit. "Song of the Lord"). The *Bhagavad Gita* is the most famous scripture of Hinduism. It is the section of the *Mahabharata* in which Krishna advises Arjuna just before a great battle.

Bhagavata Purana (lit. "Ancient Tale of the Lord"). A collection of stories of Krishna as a boy and as a youth among the cowherders.

bhakti (lit. "devotion"). The expression of an individual's faith in and love toward God.

bhakti yoga. A path to salvation consisting primarily of loving devotion to God.

Bharata. The legendary emperor from whom India took its traditional name of *Bharat*.

bharata natyam (lit. "Dance of India"). The most widely known form of the classical dance.

Bhima. The second of the Pandava brothers, heroes of the *Mahabharata* epic. Bhima was known as a fierce warrior.

Brahma. The creator-god of the *Rig Veda*. Brahma is the first of the three gods of the Hindu triad: Brahma the creator, Vishnu the preserver, and Shiva the destroyer.

brahmacharin. The first or student stage in the life of a Hindu.

Brahman. Ultimate Reality in Hindu philosophy.

Brahmins (sometimes spelled *Brahmans*). Members of the highest *varna* or occupational grouping in the caste system. The Brahmins are the priests and teachers.

Buddha. The title given to Siddhartha Gautama when he was enlightened. The Buddha was the founder of the religion called Buddhism.

buddhi (lit. "enlightened").

Buddhism. The religion which developed from the monastic community established by the Buddha in the sixth century B.C. Buddhism later spread throughout all of East and Southeast Asia, while it almost disappeared from India.

Chaitanya. A sixteenth-century Bengali saint who went into ecstasy singing the praises of Krishna.

chakra-vartin (lit. "one who turns the wheel"). The traditional title of an emperor who claimed to rule the whole world or control the "turning" of the world.

Chaulukya. A medieval dynasty of central India.

chit (lit. "pure consciousness"). With *sat* and *ananda* it is one of the three aspects of the state of final release.

Chola. A South Indian dynasty which was powerful between the ninth and twelfth centuries.

Dasharatha. Rama's father in the *Ramayana* epic.

Delhi Sultanate. Muslim dynasty which ruled India from the twelfth through the sixteenth centuries.

deva (lit. "a god"). The term *deva* is applied particularly to the gods of the *Rig Veda*.

dharma (lit. "to support"). *Dharma* refers to the proper order which supports the cosmos or society. An individual supports this order by doing his "duty" or by living righteously.

dharma shastras. Books of proper *dharma;* sacred lawbooks.

dhoti. The ordinary dress of Indian men. A *dhoti* consists of a white cloth tied around the waist and draped over the legs in a variety of fashions.

Dipavali. An alternate spelling of "Divali."

Divali. An important five-day festival in October when many lights are lit to celebrate the return of the hero of the *Ramayana,* King Rama, to his capital.

Divine Light Mission. A modern religious movement from India which has been made popular in North America by Guru Maharaj Ji.

Dravidian. A family of languages found in the four states of South India.

duhkha. Suffering or pain. This concept is especially important in Buddhism, which teaches that all of life is *duhkha.*

Durga. A goddess, the wife of Shiva. Durga is often identified with the fierce goddess Kali. She is particularly popular in Bengal.

Durvasa. The hot-tempered sage who cursed the maiden in the Shakuntala story.

Dushyanta. The king who married the maiden in the Shakuntala story.

dvara palaka (lit. "doorkeeper").

Ganapati. Another form of the name Ganesha.

Gandhi, Mohandas K. (Mahatma). The great saint and politician who led India to freedom from British rule in 1947.

Ganesha. The popular elephant-headed god. Ganesha is the son of Shiva and is known as "the remover of all obstacles." He is most popular in Maharashtra, where there is a special festival in his honor.

Ganges. The most holy river in India. The Ganges rises out of the Himalaya Mountains and then flows eastward across the great plain of northern India.

grihastha. The second or householder stage in the life of a Hindu.

Gupta. The great dynasty of medieval India which became powerful in the fourth century A.D. The Era of the Guptas was called "The Golden Age" because of their religious, cultural, and political accomplishments.

Hanuman. The monkey who helped Rama in the *Ramayana* epic. Many Hindus consider Hanuman a god.

Hare Krishna. A modern Hindu movement, based on devotion to the god Krishna, which has become popular in North America.

Holi. A popular festival, held during the spring, in which colored powder is thrown on friends and other pranks are played.

Indra. The most popular god of the *Rig Veda*. Indra is considered to be a boisterous warrior-god.

Indus Civilization. The earliest major civilization in India, flourishing about 2000 B.C. It was not discovered, however, until early in the twentieth century. The Indus Civilization was primarily agricultural, with major urban centers at Mohenjo-daro and Harappa.

Jainism. The religion started by Mahavira in the sixth century B.C. Jainism still survives in western India today.

Jatayu. An aged eagle who tried to assist Sita in the *Ramayana* epic.

jati (lit. "birth group"). The *jati* is the basic unit of the caste system. It is a group of families from among which parents select a husband or wife for their child.

jnana yoga. A path to salvation consisting primarily of "knowledge" or mystical insight, specifically, of the teachings of the *Upanishads*.

Kabir. A medieval saint who tried to reconcile Hinduism and Islam.

Kali. A fierce goddess, the wife of Shiva. Kali is often identified with the goddess Durga. She is especially popular in Bengal.

Kalidasa. A famous poet-dramatist, the author of the Shakuntala story. Kalidasa flourished around the fourth century A.D.

Kali yuga. The fourth or last age in the cycle of the world. This is the age we are presently living in.

Kama. The god of love.

Kanva. The kindly sage in the Shakuntala story.

kanyadana (lit. "the gift of a bride"). It is the duty of the parents of a girl to prepare the "giving" of their daughter in marriage.

Kanya Kumari (lit. "virgin princess"). The name for the southernmost tip of India.

karma. See *karma phalam*.

karma phalam (lit. "the fruit of one's actions"). The idea that an individual's fate or lot in this life is a result of the good or bad performed in his or her previous lives.

karma yoga. A path to salvation consisting primarily of doing good deeds and performing one's "duty."

Kartik. One of the months of the Hindu lunar calendar.

Kausalya. The mother of Rama in the *Ramayana* epic.

Krishna. The best known and most widely worshipped *avatara* (incarnation) of the god Vishnu. In some stories he is a boy and a youth playing with the cowherders. In the *Bhagavad Gita* he is the charioteer, friend, and advisor of Arjuna.

Kshatriyas. The members of the second *varna* or occupational group of the caste system. The Kshatriyas are the warriors and rulers.

Kubera. The god of wealth.

Kumbha Mela. A large festival held once every twelve years in which millions of Hindus bathe at the same time in the Ganges River. The Kumbha Mela is held in four different cities at once, but the one at Allahabad is the largest.

Kushana. A Buddhist dynasty which ruled northwest India from the first to the third century A.D.

Lakshmana. In the *Ramayana* epic, the brother of Rama.

Lakshmi. The goddess of good fortune and beauty. Lakshmi is wife of Vishnu; she is also sometimes called Shri.

lila (lit. "play"). The concept that God's activity in the world is motivated by enjoyment.

linga. The phallus. A symbolic representation of the god Shiva. This symbol is very common in temple shrines.

Mahabali. Mythological ruler of Kerala who was sent to the underworld by Vishnu. He is allowed to return to earth each year for the Onam festival, held in his honor.

Mahabharata. The *Mahabharata* and the *Ramayana* are the two great epics of India. The *Mahabharata* is the story of the great war between the Pandava brothers and their cousins. It includes the *Bhagavad Gita*.

Mahavira. The sixth-century B.C. founder of Jainism.

mandapa. A hall for marriage or for religious discourses.

mantra. Sacred verse from the ancient scriptures. If repeated silently or aloud, it is sometimes believed to have magical effects.

Manu. The best known of the ancient lawgivers of India. Manu is usually credited with defining the caste system.

marga (lit. "way"). A path to salvation, used particularly in Buddhism; Hindus generally refer to "yoga" for the same concept.

Maurya. The great dynasty which united most of India in the third century B.C. The most famous Mauryan emperor was Ashoka.

Menaka. A heavenly nymph, mother of Shakuntala.

Mesha. One of the months of the Hindu lunar calendar.

Moguls. The great Muslim dynasty which ruled India from the sixteenth to the eighteenth centuries.

moksha (lit. "release"). The final liberation from *samsara*. The ultimate state of salvation in Hinduism.

monism. The doctrine that there is only one reality, and that the impression that there are individual souls or objects separate from that reality is merely illusion.

monotheism. The doctrine that there is only one God.

Narada. A great sage of Hindu legend.

Nara-Simha (lit. "man-lion"). One of the *avataras* (incarnations) of Vishnu.

Nirvana (lit. "nonbreath, extinguishment"). In Buddhism, the state of final liberation from the world.

Onam. A festival in Kerala in which the annual return of the mythological king Mahabali takes place.

Padmini. A medieval Rajput queen.

Pala. A medieval dynasty of Bengal.

Pallava. A medieval dynasty of South India.

Panchatantra. A collection of animal stories or fables with morals attached to each.

Pandavas. The five brothers, heroes of the *Mahabharata* epic.

Pandya. A medieval dynasty of South India.

Panini. The great grammarian who lived about 300 B.C. Panini established most of the rules for the Sanskrit language.

Parvati (lit. "daughter of the mountain"). A goddess, wife of Shiva.

Patanjali. An ancient Hindu philosopher and author of the *Yoga Sutra*.

polytheism. The doctrine that there are a number of gods.

Prahlad. The son of a demon, who became famous for being a devotee of Vishnu.

prakriti (lit. "nature"). In the Samkhya school of philosophy, *prakriti* is the material half of the dualism which makes up the world.

prasada. The offering brought back from a temple which a Hindu shares with friends.

Prithivi (lit. "the broad"). The earth-goddess.

Prithvi Raj. A medieval Rajput king.

puja (lit. "worship"). Making an offering to a god in a temple or at home.

pundit. A learned man or teacher.

Puranas (lit. "ancient stories"). Texts of medieval India which contain myths about Vishnu, Shiva, and the other gods and goddesses.

purusha (lit. "man"). In the Samkhya school of philosophy, *purusha* is the spiritual half of the dualism which makes up the world.

raga. A series of notes creating a melody in Indian music.

raja. King.

rakshasas. Demons who fight against the heroes and heroines of the *Ramayana* and *Mahabharata* epics.

Rama. The hero of the *Ramayana* epic. Later, Rama was considered to be an *avatara* (incarnation) of the god Vishnu.

Ramanuja. A great Vaishnava philosopher of the twelfth century.

Rani Lakshmi Bhai. A famous queen who fought on horseback for her country.

Rashtrakuta. A medieval dynasty of central India.

Ravana. The demonic king who abducted Sita in the *Ramayana* epic.

Rig Veda. The oldest scriptures of Hinduism. A hymnbook dating to about 1500 B.C.

Roy, Ram Mohun. Nineteenth-century Hindu reformer.

sadhu. A wandering ascetic.

sahadharmini (lit. "co-worker in *dharma*"). A wife.

sakshin (lit. "witness").

Samkhya. A system of Hindu philosophy founded by the sage Kapila about 500 B.C. Samkhya says that the world is composed of two substances, *purusha* (spirit) and *prakriti* (matter).

samnyasin. A holy man who has renounced all ties with the world.

samsara. The constant change of the world; the flow of reality in which souls are continually dying and being reborn; broadly, reincarnation.

samskara (lit. "ceremony"). The series of rituals which mark an individual's passage from one stage of life to the next, from birth to death.

Samudra Gupta. The greatest of the medieval Gupta emperors.

sandhya namaskaram. Evening prayer.

Sanskrit. The classical language of India. Now it is spoken only by the learned.

saptapadi (lit. "seven steps"). An important part of the marriage ceremony.

Sarasvati. The wife of Brahma and goddess of learning.

sari. The standard dress of Indian women. It is composed of six yards of cloth wrapped carefully around the body.

sat (lit. "being"). With *chit* and *ananda* it is one of the three aspects of the state of final release.

Sena. A medieval dynasty of Bengal.

Shah Jahan. Mogul ruler who built the great Taj Mahal as a memorial to his wife.

Shaivism. The worship of the god Shiva. With Vaishnavism and Shaktism it is one of the three major religious groupings of Hinduism.

shakti (lit. "power"). The descriptive name of a goddess or the wife of a god.

Shaktism. The worship of a goddess. With Vaishnavism and Shaivism, it is one of the three major religious groupings of Hinduism.

Shakuntala. The heroine of one of India's greatest dramas.

Shankara. One of the greatest philosophers of India. Born in the eighth century, Shankara founded the school of thought known as *Advaita Vedanta,* based on the teachings of the *Upanishads.*

Shiva. One of the three major gods of Hinduism. With Brahma the creator and Vishnu the preserver, Shiva the destroyer forms the Hindu triad.

Shivaji. A Maratha hero who fought against the Muslims.

Shravana. The hermit boy accidentally killed by the king in the *Ramayana* epic.

shruti (lit. "that which is heard"). The most sacred scriptures—the *Vedas, Upanishads,* and so forth.

Shudras. Members of the fourth *varna* or occupational grouping in the caste system. The Shudras are the servants.

Shunga. Hindu dynasty which followed the Maurya.

Shurpanaka. Demoness who tried to tempt Rama in the *Ramayana* epic.

Sikhism. A religion of North India which incorporates elements of both Hinduism and Islam.

Sita. The heroine of the *Ramayana* epic.

Skanda. A warrior-god, son of Shiva.

smriti (lit. "that which is remembered"). A group of Hindu scriptures less holy than the *shruti*. The *Mahabharata* and *Ramayana* epics are examples of *smriti*.

stridhanam (lit. "wife-wealth"). Jewelry and other wealth given to a bride by her parents.

Sudaman. A famous devotee of Vishnu.

Surya. The sun god. Surya is an important god of the *Rig Veda*.

sva dharma (lit. "own duty"). An individual's awareness of his or her own role or duty in the maintenance of the order of the cosmos and of society.

svayamvara (lit. "self-choice"). An old custom by which a bride could choose a husband from among a group of suitors.

Taj Mahal. The famous memorial built by the Mogul emperor Shah Jahan in memory of his wife.

thali. A thread tied around the neck of the bride in the South Indian marriage ceremony.

Thirukkural. An ancient text on philosophy and morals from South India.

Tilak, B. G. Twentieth-century politician and Hindu thinker.

Transcendental Meditation. A modern adaptation of Hindu meditation methods which has been made popular in the West by Maharishi Mahesh Yogi.

Tulsi Das. A medieval saint who translated the *Ramayana* epic into the language of the common people.

Upanishads. Part of the sacred scriptures of Hinduism. Written about the fifth century B.C., the *Upanishads* contain some of the earliest philosophical thought of India.

Vaishnavism. With Shaivism and Shaktism, Vaishnavism is one of the three major religious groupings of Hinduism. Vaishnavism is the worship of the god Vishnu.

Vaishyas. Members of the third *varna* or occupational group of the caste system. Vaishyas are the businessmen and merchants.

Vamana. A dwarf. One of the *avataras* (incarnations) of the god Vishnu.

vanaprastha. The third stage in the life of a Hindu. In this stage, the individual becomes a "forest wanderer."

varna. A category in the caste system which identifies large occupational groups. The four *varnas* are: Brahmins (priests), Kshatriyas (warriors), Vaishyas (merchants), and Shudras (servants).

Vedanta. The philosophy of the eighth-century sage Shankara, based on the *Upanishads*.

Venkateshvara. An *avatara* (incarnation) of Vishnu.

vina. A stringed musical instrument.

Vishnu. One of the major gods of Hinduism. With Brahma the creator and Shiva the destroyer, Vishnu the preserver completes the Hindu triad.

Vivekananda. A Hindu thinker of the late nineteenth century who visited the West. Vivekananda was instrumental in reviving the popularity of Vedantic philosophy.

Vritra. In the *Rig Veda,* the enemy of the god Indra.

yoga (lit. "yoke"). A discipline or path by which an individual seeks release from the world.

Yoga Sutra. An ancient philosophical text.

Yudhishthira. In the *Mahabharata* epic, the oldest of the Pandava brothers.

yuga (lit. "age"). In ancient Hindu cosmology, a world cycle is made up of four ages. Our present age is the final one.

3. Who was Kalidasa, and what was his contribution to India? (p. 51)
4. What is the Indian word for the name *India?* (p. 55)
5. From the story of Sudaman, what is your understanding of *bhakti?* (pp. 55–56; also p. 43)
6. Explain the term *avatara* with special reference to the story of Prahlad. (pp. 56–58; also p. 24)
7. Who was Dasharatha? Why does he tell the story of Shravana to his wife during his last moments? (pp. 58–59)

FESTIVALS
1. Why are festivals important in the life of a Hindu? (p. 63)
2. Why is the New Year celebrated at different times in different places in India? (p. 63)
3. What is the religious significance of the Kumbha Mela? (p. 65)
4. Who are the following: Lakshmi, Kali, Durga, Sarasvati, Ganesha, and Hanuman? (pp. 67–68)

RELIGIOUS CEREMONIES
1. Discuss your understanding of the role of *dharma* in the life of a Hindu. (p. 68; also pp. 37–38)
2. What are the *samskaras* in the life of an individual? (p. 68)
3. Why is the marriage ceremony such an important *samskara?* (pp. 70–72)
4. What is the nature of the husband-wife relationship according to the Hindu marriage? (pp. 70–72)
5. In what ways does the Hindu marriage ceremony differ from the marriage ceremonies you are familiar with? What in your opinion is the most important difference?
6. What is a *raga?* How does dance in India differ from dance as you know it? (p. 72)

PATTERNS OF WORSHIP
1. What are the different ways in which people worship in India? (p. 74)
2. What is *prasada?* (p. 74)
3. Why are temple discourses important? As you read the passages stressing the importance of *bhakti* (devotion) and *dharma* (right living), can you think of similar passages from your own religious tradition? (p. 74)
4. What are the special occasions when *puja* (worship) is practiced at home? (p. 75)

21015-1

2. Describe the law of *karma*. Give an example of how it would affect the way a parent might answer questions children ask about the mysteries of life. (p. 34)
3. Why does consciousness have the effect of changing the human experience of the interrelatedness of life in *samsara* into an experience of life as painfulness or *duhkha?* (p. 35)
4. How would you distinguish an experience of *duhkha* from an experience of sinfulness? (p. 36)
5. Would you agree with the Buddha that careful reflection on the transcience of life ultimately leads to thinking of life as *duhkha* or painful? Explain your answer.

WHAT IS THE NATURE OF ULTIMATE REALITY?
1. Would you think there is a natural order underlying the cosmos? Underlying society? Underlying individual psychology? Why or why not?
2. Would it make moral teachings more convincing to you if they were based on the natural order as in Hinduism or on the commands of God as in Judaism, Islam, and other religions? Explain your answer.
3. When ultimate Reality is thought of as fully beyond this world, how does that affect the language people use in referring to that Reality? How does the concept of ultimate Reality make it possible for Hinduism to contain a number of different mythological systems? (pp. 38–39)
4. In what ways are the terms *monism, monotheism, polytheism,* and *animism* all partially accurate in describing the Hindu idea of God? (pp. 39–40)

WHAT IS THE WAY TO ACHIEVE SALVATION?
1. What are the three physical processes a *yogi* feels he must gain control over? (p. 42)
2. Which of the *yogas* outlined in the *Bhagavad Gita* would have the greatest appeal to you? Why? (p. 43)
3. Do you find the idea of thinking of salvation as a "release" from life pessimistic? (p. 43)
4. What are the three components of the ultimate state of salvation according to the Hindu? (p. 44)

Part III □ Practices

STORIES
1. Why is Banaras considered a holy place? (p. 47)
2. What is the *Panchatantra?* (p. 50) Can you think of any other collection of stories comparable to the *Panchatantra?*

THE HISTORY

1. Which of the two civilizations that provide the background for Indian culture worshiped fertility goddesses? (p. 14)
2. Which of the two civilizations left a book of beautiful hymns? (pp. 14–15)
3. What is the difference between *shruti* and *smriti?* (p. 18)
4. What were the Four Noble Truths taught by the Buddha? Did he have any influence on the Hindu tradition? In what ways? (pp. 18–19)
5. What was the main interest of the Upanishadic teachers? (p. 19)
6. Who are the three people who go into exile in the Ramayana story? How are they ultimately able to prevail over the forces of evil? (pp. 20–22)
7. What characteristics of Arjuna make him the central figure in the *Mahabharata* story? What is Krishna's advice to him when he hesitates to go into battle? (p. 22)
8. When was the Gupta age, and why was it considered the Golden Age of the Hindu tradition? (p. 23)
9. What was the *avatara* concept in the system of worship associated with Vishnu? How did it allow the sect associated with Vishnu to include a variety of popular gods in one system? (p. 24)
10. Who are the two sons of Shiva? (p. 24)
11. Who was Ramanuja, and how did his philosophy differ from that of Shankara? (p. 26) Which philosophy would you think was more like Christian thought?
12. How were the Mogul rulers different from the rulers of the Delhi Sultanate which preceded them? (p. 27)
13. Who built the Taj Mahal? (p. 27)
14. Why do you think the British rulers might have thought that Indian culture was morally inferior? Do you think that kind of judgment was justified?
15. Why do you think a political leader such as Gandhi could come to be thought of as a religious figure by Hindus? Could there be a parallel to that in any Western nation?
16. From what you know about Transcendental Moditation or the Hare Krishna movement, do you think they are good representations of Hinduism?

Part II □ Ideas

WHAT IS THE NATURE OF HUMAN EXPERIENCE?

1. What attitudes toward ecology do you think people might develop from the idea of *samsara?* (p. 33)

Study Questions
for
Hinduism

The following are suggested study questions for a classroom study
of *Hinduism* by Paul Younger and Susanna Oommen Younger.
Questions based directly on the text are followed by page references
that indicate the pages on which the relevant discussion may be found.

Part I □ Traditions

THE LAND

1. What are the six countries that surround India in the subcontinent
   of South Asia? (p. 5) The authors say that these countries have
   religious loyalties somewhat different from those of India.
   Do you know the religions followed by the majority of the people
   in these six countries? (Afghanistan, Pakistan, and Bangladesh
   are predominantly Islamic; Nepal, Sri Lanka, and Burma are
   predominantly Buddhist.)
2. What are the major mountain systems of India? (p. 6) What do
   mountains and forests symbolize to Hindus? (p. 7)
3. What are the major river valleys of India? Why are the rivers
   considered holy? Which is considered the holiest? (pp. 6–7)
4. Why have the subregions of India been able to maintain such
   distinctive subcultures? (p. 7)
5. What are the five major regions of India? Name at least one
   distinctive characteristic of each. (p. 8)
6. Have the students fill in blank maps of India showing (a) the
   mountains, (b) the rivers, (c) the regions, and (d) the rainfall pattern.

THE SOCIAL ORDER

1. What is a *jati?* (p. 10)
2. What are some occupations which Hindus would consider very
   unclean? (p. 11) How does their idea of "unclean" differ from that of
   a Westerner?
3. What are the three *varnas* the lawgiver Manu thought should be
   ranked first? (p. 12)
4. What is the difference between *sadhus* and *samnyasins?* (p. 12)
5. How does having a hierarchical society help an individual
   understand the stages in his or her spiritual quest better? (p. 12)
6. Why do you think North American society strives for equality? Is that
   a more natural way to organize a human society, or is the Indian
   hierarchy a more natural way? Explain your answer.